NUTRITION · NEW STORY · NEW YOU

COOKBOOK

Delicious recipes and your guide to avoiding the common pitfalls of the AIP diet

CLAIRE SMEDLEY · SUE PERSAD-PATEL

NUTRITION · NEW STORY · NEW YOU: **COOKBOOK**

To contact the publisher:
www.clairesmedleyhealthcoaching.com

To contact the authors:
clairesmedleyhealth@gmail.com
aipcookingwithsue@gmail.com

PHOTOGRAPHY: Sue Persad-Patel and Claire Smedley
BOOK DESIGN: Melina Lew

ISBN: 978-1-7396818-0-7
Printed in the United Kingdom

We dedicate this book to all those seeking the inspiration to achieve healing through food.

We wish you an abundance of health and joy

Contents

INTRODUCTION

Claire's Story

I will never forget the moment when I received my blood test results and my doctor told me I had the autoimmune disease, Hashimoto's Thyroiditis. I found myself in a turmoil of conflicting emotions for days. They went from "great—I have a diagnosis" to "how did this happen to me? I live a healthy lifestyle!" to "is this how I am going to feel forever?" and just about everything else in between.

To then be told that there was nothing I could do to manage my symptoms myself and I would need to take medication for the rest of my life, was utterly soul-destroying. After all, I had spent the last 2 decades living a natural lifestyle and teaching others to do the same. Surely, there must be something I could do? And in the darkest moments I asked "what did I do wrong? Why is this happening to me? What a fraud, I have been teaching healthy living all these years".

I was always a stubborn wench, so I set off on a research journey of my own and I am so glad I did—clearly my stubborn nature was a gift after all! I discovered a lot about myself and how putting my needs last for years, had been at my own expense and now it was taking its toll. I would work 7 days a week for weeks on end, seize up and feel exhausted and take just enough time to rest and "restore" myself as I could get away with. The moment I felt alright again, I would be back to the same old destructive pattern of striving. I existed in a loop of being too busy, collapse in a heap, rest a bit and start the loop all over again.

The other great thing I learned from all the science out there, was that my "healthy" diet was in fact not healthy for me (or for the millions of people like me).

I decided to experiment with the Autoimmune Paleo approach to eating (also called the Autoimmune Protocol or AIP) and went all in. By following it, I reversed all of my symptoms.

I said goodbye to constant fatigue, brain fog, weight gain, hair loss, depression, anxiety, high cholesterol, irritable bowel syndrome, constipation, always being cold and rediscovered my joy for life. I was so impressed by my results that I trained as an Integrative Nutrition Health Coach with advanced studies in Gut Health and became a certified AIP Coach. This was a perfect fit with my 20+ years as a Yoga and Meditation Teacher.

I utilised Nutrition (AIP) and Lifestyle (yoga, meditation and mindset work) married together for the perfect healing package to tame my overactive immune system, reduce inflammation, heal my gut and free myself from limiting beliefs that kept me stuck in repetitive patterns. I had suffered with IBS for 30 years and finally I found a way of eating and living that really got this under control and got my cholesterol levels in the normal range for the first time in 30 years of tracking it. Feeling so much better, there would be no more putting myself at the bottom of the list.

There's nothing unique about my story or about me: if I can do this, so can you. I know that to be an absolute truth.

Changing how you eat and how you live is not easy and having guided many women through the AIP diet as part of the process to reclaim their health, I find the same stumbling blocks come up over, and over again for most people. I narrowed it down to 5 main issues and that's why I was compelled to write this book to help you, the reader, have an easier transition to better health.

Eating this way can be creative and delicious, packed with variety and flavour, or it can be dull, repetitive and feel like punishment. You get to choose!

As well as an understanding of the AIP diet and plenty of scrumptious recipes you'll be happy to eat forever, this book will help you navigate the 5 main obstacles and reframe your mindset so you love the way you nourish your body.

In Part 1 you'll learn the fundamentals of the diet—what you can and can't eat as well as the process of reintroducing foods until you have a bespoke, health-building diet, totally unique to you. Don't worry though, it does NOT mean you are forever doomed to eat alone—far from it!

Part 2 is where we trouble-shoot the 5 big obstacles:

1 The importance of being prepared
2 What on earth am I going to eat for breakfast?
3 Is my food going to be boring and bland forever?
4 How can I eat this way and still enjoy food with others?
5 Reframing the process from restriction to nourishment, from punishment to self-love

If you are already familiar with the AIP way but have fallen off the wagon when you've tried it before, then feel free to jump straight into Part 2. See which of these obstacles tripped you up in the past, so you can be better equipped when you try the approach again.

And the final part, Part 3, is where you will find delicious and fool-proof recipes to flood your body with nutrients and flavour galore. I love food, I love flavour and in order to make permanent changes to the way I eat, I didn't want to compromise on that. Our recipes address the common obstacles outlined in Part 2 so that transitioning to this way of eating is easier and tastier than you might think.

Even if you don't suffer from an autoimmune disease but are simply looking for delicious and health-promoting recipes, then the recipes in this book will not let you down.

I am on a mission to help women remove everything that prevents them from living a life of fulfilment and purpose. We start with the basics - physical and mental health, then the heart's desire can shine forth into a life of purpose and satisfaction, but I'll save that for another book!

Sue's Story

When my children were very young, I started suffering from initial symptoms of fatigue, not really understanding what it was. I honestly felt that most people must feel this exhausted after having children, experiencing sleepless nights and managing a busy job. I simply existed and survived each week, picking up every bug that came my way, keeping my head just above water with my low energy, fatigue, pain, poor sleep and concentration. Instead of having the energy to do fun things as a family and socialising at weekends, for me it was all about trying to rest and conserve energy, so I would be able to function again the week after.

After a couple of years with periods of struggle and higher levels of fatigue, I hit a low point and was diagnosed with a condition suspected of being autoimmune in nature—Chronic Fatigue Syndrome. To be told at that point that there was no medication was so disheartening and I literally had no idea how to manage it. I was left feeling lost and completely alone.

Since then, I have gradually tried to manage my symptoms with the small amounts of exercise I could cope with, keeping social commitments to a minimum, cutting out alcohol and caffeine and eating low carbs and fats—what I thought was a 'healthy' way of eating for my body. Despite this, the sleep problems, fatigue, pain and brain fog continued. I managed to function under the radar until I hit an incredibly stressful period in my life. The physical symptoms of stress that I experienced left me with anxiety and brought back a Chronic Fatigue crash with a vengeance.

My journey to the Autoimmune Protocol or AIP was a call that changes were imperative in my lifestyle, mental and physical health. I had not listened to the warning signs for so long, instead convincing myself that I was doing ok. My mind and body had hit rock bottom and my autoimmune condition had awoken again. I started the process of trying to rest, heal and manage the extreme fatigue and pain. I asked the universe for help and that's how the angel that is Rachel appeared. She introduced me to a whole new world of magical essential oils and practices I wanted to immerse myself in. It was my time and the universe had listened and showed me which path I needed to take. From there, the more Rachel shared, the more I wanted to learn and when she told me how Claire's AIP and lifestyle program had changed her life, I was incredibly intrigued.

I was introduced to the wonderful Claire and I honestly felt like the AIP nutrition and lifestyle program she had designed was written specifically for me. I had finally found my way to a healthy mind and body and all of the answers I had been searching for, for so long were waiting for me within the program.

Food has always formed such a huge part of my life. Growing up, flavoursome food was always at the centre of all our family gatherings and being totally honest, at first, the thought of the elimination phase really concerned me. These worries quickly disappeared as the elimination phase made me feel so much healthier, sleep better and even dream again! The constant feeling of extreme fatigue and brain fog improved and the daily pain I had been living with reduced. I lost weight without even trying and I eat so much more now.

During the elimination phase I found that my thoughts and dreams were consumed with food and so many tasty AIP recipes I wanted to create and eat. I have always been a creative being at heart, but I felt like a fire had been ignited inside me again, reawakening my flair for cooking new foods. I began creating, cooking and photographing my creations and that is how Claire asked me to join her in co-writing this amazing book. The prospect of collaborating on this book felt so exciting and inspirational to me that it literally made me jump for joy. I can honestly say that eating AIP is so tasty, satisfying, exciting and liberating. This book will provide you with the approach and fundamentals of the AIP diet and so many delicious dishes that will leave you feeling truly satisfied.

With my newfound energy there is nothing more that I want than to use my creativity and passion to help others suffering from debilitating chronic illnesses and this cookbook really has the potential to do just this. I genuinely hope the recipes we have created and poured our love into will help you to feel inspired to cook exciting and mouth-watering food that will positively change your life.

We are both so delighted you have picked up this book, you might just look back upon this moment one day and see it as a major turning point in your life.

So, ready to dive in, get prepared and get cooking?

PART 1

AUTOIMMUNITY & THE PATH TO HEALING

CHAPTER 1

Some Background into Autoimmunity

Before the beginning of agriculture, human beings were hunter-gatherers. They lived in harmony and in tune with the natural world around them and they depended on the environment to meet all their dietary and medicinal needs.

We have moved on socially in leaps and bounds since then, but we have become more and more separated from the sources of our food and healing. Whilst we have evolved socially, biologically we have hardly changed at all since those hunter-gatherer times.

Our biology is struggling with the modern diet and modern farming practices. So much of our food is a chemical mush, produced in factories, highly processed and addictive. I often wonder what our ancestors would make of the things we call "food" these days. Much of it is slowly poisoning us and robbing us of the vibrant health we were born with.

The modern diet is driving key health epidemics like obesity, diabetes, gut dysfunction and autoimmunity by creating an internal environment of inflammation and nutrient insufficiency. We know that inflammation is a key symptom in almost all chronic illness and diet is one of the main culprits.

The food we put in our mouth, however, is only one part of the problem. We also have a mental diet that is out of control. Modern life is stressful, with the added societal obsession for comparing ourselves with others. We worry, we fear, we bury away our traumas so we can just keep going. Stress is another key driver of inflammation. Taken together with poor nutrition we really have created a civilisation of suffering.

But there is good news because both nutrition and developing the ability to respond well to stress (because it isn't going to ever go away) are within our daily control. In this book we'll be focusing primarily on restoring good nutrition as a place to start.

The Paleo diet is a pre-agricultural, ancestral diet, meaning a return to the way our ancient ancestors ate, a time when chronic illness and many of the diseases of the modern world were unheard of.

For the purpose of autoimmune healing, the Paleo diet has been further modified to be even more targeted at reducing inflammation, providing the body with all the nutrients it needs to regulate the immune system and repair damaged tissues. This modified version is known as **The Autoimmune Paleo diet (AIP)**.

In her phenomenal book "The Paleo Approach" Sarah Ballantyne PhD sets out the science behind what is going wrong in our body when we have autoimmune disease and how food contributes either to symptoms or to healing. I highly recommend reading it if you are a science fanatic like me, however, if even the thought of complex science sends your brain into a fog, rest assured, this book will be less about the "how" it works and more about implementing the AIP diet in a way that sets you up for success and better health. After all, knowledge is NOT power, implemented knowledge is.

We do need to set out a few fundamentals though, so here goes. Firstly, there is a difference between nutrient *deficiency* and nutrient *insufficiency*. Full blown nutrient deficiencies lead to recognisable diseases, such as beri-beri, scurvy and rickets. Very few people have these, but that does not necessarily mean people are eating enough nutrient-rich food to have sufficient nutrients for all the things the body needs to do. This leads to a grey area of **nutrient insufficiency**. A key, but often neglected component when implementing the AIP diet, is making sure we flood the body with nutrients.

The immune system is one of the biggest consumers of vitamins and other essential nutrients. In autoimmune disease, the immune system doesn't regulate itself properly and in effect, remains switched on 24/7, requiring even more nutrients than a person with a balanced and healthy immune system. A dysregulated immune system drives chronic inflammation and is the beginning of all the symptoms which follow.

Stress also leads to more rapid depletion of key immune-supporting nutrients such as Vitamin C. So, when you are going through stressful phases in your life, you actually need to be eating more nutrient-rich food. The reality when stress hits, is we often turn to high sugar, high fat and nutrient poor foods, making the whole thing spiral downwards.

One way to think about your immune system is that it is like your internal army, defending your body against invaders and anything which shouldn't get in. Now imagine you send that army out without adequate kit—no weapons, boots or vehicles. How well do you think that army would perform against the opposition? Not very well and this can manifest in you as always picking up all the coughs and colds that are going around.

Now imagine that the under-resourced army isn't allowed to rest either. Instead, it is expected to fight throughout the day and night, week after week. They are going to need even more resources AND they are going to get tired. What happens when you are tired at work but have to keep going? You make mistakes. Your immune system does too—it starts to misidentify healthy tissues which are part of you as invaders and starts to attack those healthy tissues as well.

So, the key point here is: we have to equip our immune system with what it needs to function at its best and regulate itself, and that means nutrients.

The second key part of the approach is we need to stop giving the immune system so much to fight in the first place. Your skin, and this includes the lining of your gut from mouth to anus, provides a boundary between you and the outside world. It can be a hard concept to grasp but the contents of the tube of your gut from one end to the other is EXTERNAL to you. You are basically an elongated ring donut with arms and legs. Anything in the gut tube must first pass across the gut lining and into the bloodstream to be INSIDE you.

Think of this skin layer like the borders of an island you live on. Where would you exert the most effort to stop invaders from getting onto your island? At the borders and main ports of entry. So, it won't surprise you to learn that 80% of all your immune function happens along the lining of your gut. It's a huge surface to protect and there is a high risk of pathogens arriving with every meal.

Immune function and gut health go hand in hand. With poor diet, poor sleep, unmanaged stress & anxiety, as well as some medications, the health of our gut takes a hammering. The gut lining becomes damaged, does not repair fully and starts to become too permeable, known commonly as a **Leaky Gut**. Instead of just letting through health-providing nutrients, the gut now allows larger particles, pathogens, partially digested foods, toxins and other foreign substances to pass across the barrier. Your immune system is there waiting but it quickly gets overwhelmed, and these substances get into the body where they shouldn't be.

Nature, whether it's plants or animals, is made up from the same building blocks as we are—proteins. The immune system sees a semi-digested protein as a potentially harmful invader, such as a bacteria and works to destroy it. It then encounters the same partial protein in our own healthy tissue, thinks it's a problem too and begins to destroy that as well. Over time this results in tissue damage and lack of function.

It's not helpful or conducive to healing to berate your immune system for "attacking" you as if you are the victim here. Your immune system is under-resourced, exhausted and overwhelmed. Despite these shoddy working conditions, it's doing its best to protect you. Now it's time for you to stop giving it so much to fight and instead give it what it needs to do its job better and more accurately.

How does Autoimmune Disease start?

Why do some people get an autoimmune disease whilst others are spared? It has become clear that there are several factors that need to be in place for an autoimmune disease to appear:

1 First there is a leaky gut. Whenever this has been looked for in an autoimmune patient it has been found to be present. Leaky gut is now being considered the precursor to autoimmunity.

2 There is also a genetic predisposition for autoimmunity. Autoimmune disease does seem to run in families but not necessarily the same disease. For example, your mother may have Hashimoto's Thyroiditis, your grandmother had Lupus and you suffer from Rheumatoid Arthritis. These may seem like completely different diseases, but they are all autoimmune and begin through the same pathways.

3 Finally, there must be a trigger to set the immune system and inflammation into overdrive. This can be a toxin exposure, infection, stress of high intensity or long duration, a traumatic event or other emotionally-charged situation.

Whilst we can't change our genetics, science is showing us that we can influence which genes are active in our bodies and which lie dormant (the field of science called epigenetics). We can exert the greatest influence over this gene expression through our nutrition and lifestyle choices. So that's the good news or the bad news depending on your chosen perspective—it's in your hands to influence this if you decide to.

Even if you have autoimmune disease in your family, by keeping your gut in good shape, avoiding a leaky gut and the inflammation which follows, and intentionally managing your stress, you have a much higher chance of NOT developing an autoimmune disease.

Once you have one autoimmune disease, without addressing diet and lifestyle, you are three times more likely than the general population to develop another. It is not uncommon to meet people who have 5+ autoimmune diagnoses who are continuing to add to their list.

Getting a diagnosis can often take many years and visits to many different health care professionals. You don't need to wait for a diagnosis to start feeling better. Indeed, if autoimmune disease is present in your family, by proactively eating the AIP way before any symptoms arise, you can have a very big impact on whether or not you will develop one at all. Don't wait until it hits you to make changes.

An article in the journal *Scientific American* in 2021 estimated that 4.5% of the world's population have an autoimmune disease. We are almost at 8 billion people on our planet, so this equates to a staggering **360 million** people. This is a human catastrophy, largely avoidable.

Occurances of Common Autoimmune Diseases

DISEASE	OCCURANCE*	GENDER
Psoriasis	>1 in 100	Affects both equally
Hashimoto's Thyroiditis	1 in 100	Predominantly women
Coeliac	1 in 100	Affects both equally
Graves'	1 in 100	Predominantly women
Rheumatoid Arthritis	1 in 100	Predominantly women
Type 1 Diabetes	1 in 1,000	Slightly more men than women
Vitiligo	1 in 1,000	Affects both equally
Alopecia Areata	1 in 1,000	Affects both equally
Multiple Sclerosis	1 in 1,000	Slightly more women than men
Systemic Lupus Erythrematosis (SLE)	1 in 10,000	Predominantly women
Ulcerative Colitis	1 in 10,000	Slightly more women than men
Crohn's	1 in 10,000	Slightly more men than women
Scleroderma	1 in 10,000	Predominantly women
Sjogren's Syndrome	1 in 10,000	Predominantly women

Abridged version of *Scientific American* article, 2021

Currently, there are approximately 100 recognised autoimmune diseases, ranging from the very rare to very common and another 40 diseases being investigated as having an autoimmune component.

Autoimmunity affects predominantly women (approx. 85% on average) but it does vary by disease. Age of onset also varies from childhood to age 40–50 and older.

Some common diseases which are suspected of being autoimmune in nature include Fibromyalgia, Myalgic Encephalomyelitis/Chronic Fatigue Syndrome (ME/CFS), Type 2 Diabetes and recently, Long COVID.

All of these diseases can benefit from following the AIP diet.

Depending on which parts of the body the immune system is targeting will give rise to the particular symptoms associated with that disease. However, there are symptoms which are common across many different diseases, associated with a dysfunctional gut and systemic inflammation. Some of the common symptoms I encounter with clients include:

- Fatigue (not to be confused with tiredness which is remedied by sleep)
- General pain (including headaches and migraines, joint and muscle pain)
- Skin irritations and rashes
- Hair loss
- Depression and a sense of hopelessness
- Anxiety
- Insomnia
- Brain fog, lack of concentration and mental fatigue

When you heal your gut, give your body the nutrition it needs to thrive and implement daily stress reduction practices many of these symptoms diminish or even disappear altogether.

If you are interested in how to manage your symptoms through great nutrition then read on. It works well alongside prescription medication but be sure to talk to your doctor before embarking on any change to your diet in case of any possible implications. As your health improves, your doctor may decide to adjust your medication levels accordingly. Take this book with you to your next appointment so they know exactly what you plan to change.

CHAPTER 2

Phases of the Autoimmune Paleo Diet

It is one of the most common pitfalls to become overly-focused on what this diet asks you to remove and it will feel like a punishment if you only focus here (see later chapters on the 5 key obstacles). In reality, there are three intentions with the AIP diet and all need an equal focus:

Heal the Gut

You need to close the holes in the most important boundary you have between you and the outside world. The gut lining is only one cell thick and very delicate. Compare that with our external skin which is about 2mm thick and fairly robust. The gut lining can easily get damaged and become more porous. If we make no attempt to repair this, foreign particles will continue to enter the body and the immune system will always have something to fight.

Some foods help repair the damaged gut lining and these foods will be emphasised.

The quality, diversity and types of bacteria which live in the gut are also critical to keeping the gut lining healthy. Including probiotic foods and supplements is an important part of gut healing, especially if you have a history of antibiotic use.

Stress contributes to a leaky gut as well, so incorporating daily stress-resilience techniques such as yoga, meditation, a gratitude practice, exercise and being in nature are an important part of your recovery and not to be skipped.

Remove Inflammatory and Gut-Irritating Foods

Many foods which we might consider healthy, such as legumes and seeds, are excluded for a period of time. This enables the gut to heal and for inflammation to calm down. These foods, whilst they have nutritional value, also contain some compounds known to aggravate an already irritated gut (see Appendix 2 for the nutritional reasons behind these exclusions).

Once symptoms have significantly improved (how long this takes varies from person to person) we would introduce these foods back into the diet for more variety, so long as they are well tolerated.

Some foods however, are known to drive inflammation and we would not be looking to bring these back in, especially in large quantities. Foods in this category include sugar, processed foods, seed and vegetable oils and some grains.

Finally, there are foods which will trigger symptoms in you but are fine for someone else. As you reintroduce foods you will discover these problem foods and I am sure you will want to avoid them altogether because once you are used to feeling good, you will not want to go back.

In the end you will have a bespoke nutritional plan that works for you. This will empower you to be in control of how you nourish your body and manage your condition. (Full details for creating your personal nutritional program is covered in the following chapters).

Flood the Body with Nutrients

You need to give the body what it needs to return to balance, repair damage and continue to keep out anything harmful. It's not enough to just cut out harmful foods (plus it's boring and will feel like punishment). The emphasis at each meal is to start by including the good stuff—fill your plate with foods known to be nutrient dense and foods known to be anti-inflammatory in nature, so you get more nutrition per mouthful. This principle is called "Crowding Out". By focusing on what you want to increase on our plate, you naturally and effortlessly, leave less room for what you don't want.

Many of the people I have worked with have grown to love eating this way. The vast majority of them say they couldn't imagine going back to how they used to eat and almost all of them discover a joy of cooking, preparing and even growing their own food again. They eat more variety and flavour and serve up food that can be enjoyed by the whole family. After all, we know there is a genetic component to autoimmune disease, so the sooner your children can embrace a health-promoting, anti-inflammatory diet the better. If they can avoid developing a leaky gut, they increase their chances of avoiding chronic illness altogether.

There is nothing weird or restrictive about this way of eating unless you decide there is. This is the way our ancient ancestors ate from the environment around them, gaining all their needs for health and vitality. This is the way we are biologically designed to eat for optimal health and function and it can also be delicious as you will see in the recipes in Part 3.

Keep these three intentions in mind as we now explore the four phases of the AIP diet:

Preparation Phase

In phase 1, you will be getting the kitchen and the family ready for your new way of eating. This might include:

- meal planning
- shopping for new ingredients to stock the pantry
- picking up some new equipment
- donating food items you don't want lying around to tempt you
- batch cooking some meals to freeze for emergencies and
- beginning to keep track of your food and symptoms in a journal

Time spent planning will make the transition much easier than diving right in. I cannot emphasise this phase enough for a seamless transition.

Elimination Phase

I sometimes refer to this as the Repair Phase—during this phase, which can last 30–90 days, or longer depending on the severity of your symptoms, you will be 100% compliant with the foods to avoid and foods to include. It is during this time that the gut heals and you will start to experience a reduction (or even a complete removal) of your symptoms. Many people start with the new diet all at once. However, if the thought of that alarms you, you can transition more slowly, over a few weeks, by removing a proportion of the eliminated foods each week and adding in the new foods over this period as well. Once you are eating in a fully AIP-compliant way, continue for at least 30 days and track your symptoms.

I encourage you to keep a food diary throughout this process and track your symptoms. If you do not start to feel better, there may be particular foods which, although allowed on the AIP diet, are not tolerated very well by you. We are all individual and being able to link your symptoms to particular foods will help you identify any additional modifications you need to make.

Reintroduction Phase

This is where you will be able to reintroduce foods one by one, whilst keeping track of your symptom changes. The goal of the AIP Elimination and Reintroduction Diet is to help you identify your personal food triggers and eliminate those, ultimately eating as much variety as possible with the fewest symptoms.

Maintenance Phase

Once you have tested all the foods you want to reintroduce and have determined which foods your body doesn't tolerate well, you will end up with a bespoke and more varied diet. It's important to continue with the idea of "crowding out"—continue to eat the nutrient dense foods you emphasised during the repair phase and add foods to this, rather than switching back to old habits of eating which can send you back into nutrient insufficiency and symptoms again.

There is no cure for autoimmune disease—once the immune system has learned to attack certain tissues, it cannot unlearn it. By continuing to enjoy the recipes in this book plus the additions your body tolerates, you can keep symptoms at bay and flares to a minimum. P.S. Don't ignore stress! Diet alone is not strong enough to avoid flares if your stress is through the roof.

CHAPTER 3

The Preparation Phase

I cannot emphasise enough the importance of spending time getting prepared. Your transition will go more smoothly if you spend a good week or 10 days getting organised and ready to begin eating in a new way. When I work with clients, I often have to coach people not to dive straight in and go off half-prepared. All this does is create questions and obstacles further down the road, a pattern of constantly trouble-shooting issues as they arise and lots of frustration.

As someone who loves jumping into things, I really understand the urge to get going but trust me on this—you are setting yourself up for a miserable time. Use the first week or two to get all your ducks in a row.

In the Beginning Spend 1–2 Weeks Getting Prepared to Start

It may not be what you want to hear, but honestly this is my top tip with transitioning to eating the AIP way. It takes away most of the potential obstacles you'll meet along the way before you even begin.

So, in the first couple of weeks I recommend the following:

Get the kitchen on your side

Take time to highlight all the allowed foods you are encouraged to emphasise during the elimination phase that you either already eat, or you at least like. Either write in this book, photocopy the list or write your own list in a journal or on your phone.

Check the list of foods you will be avoiding. Are there items on the list you know you will never eat again? Maybe you have decided as part of a long-term approach to good nutrition that you will no longer eat processed foods, sugar, refined grains or processed vegetable oils.

In this case, review your pantry, fridge and freezer and remove all these items. Donate them to your local food bank if they are unopened and still in date. Discard or eat up everything else.

If you have family members who will continue to eat these foods, you may want to give yourself a designated cupboard so you won't be tempted to reach for these convenient but nutritionally bereft foods in an emergency. Don't worry—if you follow the tips in this book, you won't have any emergencies, but I advise, as much as possible, to get these "never again" foods out of the house, or at least out of view.

There will be another group of foods which you will be excluding for a while but will want to reintroduce them at some point because they are nutritionally valuable. Foods such as beans, nuts and seeds, for example.

Check the dates on these foods to see if they will still be edible in 2–3 months' time. If not, again either donate them or eat them up before you begin. For those foods which will still be in date, place them somewhere inaccessible, such as the top shelf of the cupboard. Being only 5 feet 3, all the top shelves are inaccessible for me but if you think you'll still be able to see them and be tempted, I suggest you box them up and place them in the garage or loft for later.

Whilst you are detoxing the kitchen, continue to eat as you were but when shopping for groceries, start selecting from the allowed list so you are already incorporating more of these nutritious foods into your diet. This is a little like a soft launch. You will already be starting to eat these foods more regularly, as you finish off some of the foods you are clearing out of the cupboards and freezer.

All of this can happen slowly over the first week or two.

As you will be cooking most of your food yourself, rather than eating pre-prepared, restaurant or takeaway food, it's important to check your kitchen equipment is up to the task. Suggested basic items include:

- Chopping boards
- Sharp knives
- Mixing bowls of various sizes
- Storage containers – ideally glass rather than plastic if possible, and freezer-safe

- Hand blender
- Measuring cups and spoons
- Roasting tin
- Wok or large non-stick frying pan
- Slow cooker

Purchase what you need and remember they don't need to be fancy or expensive, they just need to do the job.

Stock up on staples

Many of the recipes in this book use some key ingredients over and over again, which you may not be familiar with—yet! They provide easy replacements for some of the staple ingredients you already rely on. I consider the following ingredients must-have items in an AIP kitchen:

- Apple cider vinegar
- Arrowroot flour
- Avocado oil
- Cassava flour
- Coconut aminos
- Coconut milk
- Coconut oil
- Extra virgin olive oil
- Garlic
- Ginger (fresh and powdered)
- Lemongrass
- Lemons and limes
- Maple syrup
- Medjool dates...for when you need a sweet treat
- Onions (red and brown)
- Salt (sea salt or pink Himalayan salt)
- Selection of dried herbs
- Selection of herbal or fruit teas
- Selection of powdered spices including cinnamon and turmeric
- Tinned mackerel (in brine, spring water or olive oil)
- Tinned sardines (in brine, spring water or olive oil)
- Tinned tuna (in brine, spring water or olive oil)

Wean off coffee during this time

Many of the foods you will be taking out during the elimination/repair phase are addictive in nature. They literally light up the pleasure centres of the brain and leave you wanting more. These foods include sugar, refined carbohydrates and dairy products. When we stop eating these foods, we can experience detox and withdrawal symptoms such as headache, fatigue and a general increase in our autoimmune symptoms. Many people panic and think the AIP approach isn't working for them, but rest assured this is normal and only lasts a few days.

Try to ensure that you start the diet when you have time to take life a little more slowly, rest more for those first few days and drink lots of water—more than you normally would.

Then we have coffee.

I only drank one cup of coffee a day and didn't think I was "addicted" but I still experienced headaches when I cut the coffee out. Rather than have this withdrawal at the same time as everything else, my advice is to wean yourself off this in the preparation weeks.

I recommend the following two approaches, depending on how much coffee you currently drink:

5-Day Approach

- Day 1: 2 cups coffee
- Day 2: 1 cup coffee (replace the other with tea: black, green, fruit, or herbal)
- Day 3: ½ cup coffee (replace the other again with tea if required)
- Day 4: ¼ cup coffee
- Day 5: zero coffee

3-Day Approach

- Day 1: 1 cup 50% decaf and 50% regular coffee
- Day 2: 1 cup 100% decaf coffee
- Day 3: zero coffee

The AIP protocol is not a caffeine-free diet but it is a coffee-bean-free diet. You can continue to enjoy black tea and green tea in moderation, without milk. Try a slice of lemon or coconut milk in your tea if you find tea without cow's milk not to your taste.

Pick your start date at least three days away

Once you have prepared the kitchen, next pick a start date when you will begin the elimination phase and put it in your diary. Make sure all your family members know this is happening and reassure them they will still be able to eat what they want— this is your journey. More on navigating eating with others in Part 2.

Creating a meal plan, shopping for it and preparing food in advance is a weekly routine and not just for the start of the journey. Full tips are covered in Chapter 7. With a weekly routine you can save so much time and stress.

CHAPTER 4

The Elimination Phase

Once you are prepared and ready to go, the elimination phase begins. This is where you start eating in a new, anti-inflammatory and healing way.

Removing problem foods

These are foods which are difficult to digest, feed pathogenic bacteria and yeast, stimulate the immune system into an inflammatory state, drive insulin resistance and damage the delicate gut lining. For a minimum of 30 days you remove these elements from the diet. Some people will remain in this phase for longer. How long you remain here will depend on your symptoms, not the calendar and it's important to keep track of the food you eat and any symptoms you experience.

Repairing the gut lining and rebuilding the colony of beneficial bacteria

This can take some time, depending on the amount of damage and "leakiness" that is present. How will you know when the gut is healed? You will experience a decrease in symptoms such as bloating, cramping, indigestion, reflux, diarrhoea and constipation and return to a rhythm of daily, well-formed bowel movements.

Since mood is significantly influenced by gut health, you may start to feel less anxiety and depression and feel more positive and motivated.

As your diet naturally switches from foods which pathogenic bacteria and yeast like to consume (such as sugar and grains) to foods which your beneficial bacteria thrive on (such as vegetables) the microbiome will start to alter. Include probiotic foods into the diet or supplement with them.

Flooding the body with the nutrients and building blocks it needs to function optimally

As I said in Chapter 2, it's not enough to remove problem foods. The body needs resources to repair damaged tissues and regulate the immune system. There are foods to be included on a regular basis and these may not be foods you currently cook or eat.

We emphasise foods which are anti-inflammatory, nutrient dense and contain few, if any, gut-irritating compounds.

Tissue damage may be widespread or specific to certain areas depending on the nature of your autoimmune disease. For example, if you have Rheumatoid Arthritis there will be damage in the joints, if you have Hashimoto's Thyroiditis the damage will primarily be in the thyroid gland. The more damage present (which can be due to the length of time you have been living with your condition) the more nutrient dense foods you will need and possibly for a longer period of time.

There will undoubtedly be damage to the gut (even if you experience no obvious gut symptoms) as this goes hand in hand with autoimmune disease and is often made worse by prescription medications. Your new way of eating will include some very specific foods known to heal the gut lining, such as bone broth.

So, let's dive in and see what you can and can't have during the elimination phase. But remember, this phase is temporary, you will be adding foods back in that your body can tolerate once you have experienced a measurable reduction in your symptoms, particularly gut-related symptoms.

This is a nutrient-rich phase and will form the backbone of your dietary needs going forward, together with some reintroductions.

Be sure to read the chapters on the common obstacles before you start changing anything, so you are set up for success.

Building Your Meals—The AIP Plate Guide

You may be an experimental cook, you may be a novice and feel that following recipes is the best way for you to approach this transition. Either way, this visual can be a quick and easy check to see if the majority of your meals are giving you the balanced nutrition you need to thrive.

You can also use this template to construct meals you love, from ingredients which are readily available in your area and in your budget.

Building your plate with this template takes so much of the stress away when trying to figure out what to eat. Using the principle of "Crowding out" you fill the plate with the foods you are choosing to emphasise, leaving little room for the old offenders.

As you can see, half of your plate is filled up with vegetables, about a quarter is starchy vegetables, such as root vegetables and squashes and the remaining quarter is animal/fish protein.

Fruit is allowed, but not in the same quantities as vegetables and a small amount of healthy fat is also required.

The list of foods which follows is colour-coded to match this plate for easy reference—pick something from each colour list and eat a rainbow! Even when you have a snack it's a good idea to include a little protein, such as some pate or left-over chicken especially if you need to stabilise your blood sugar and to avoid sugar cravings.

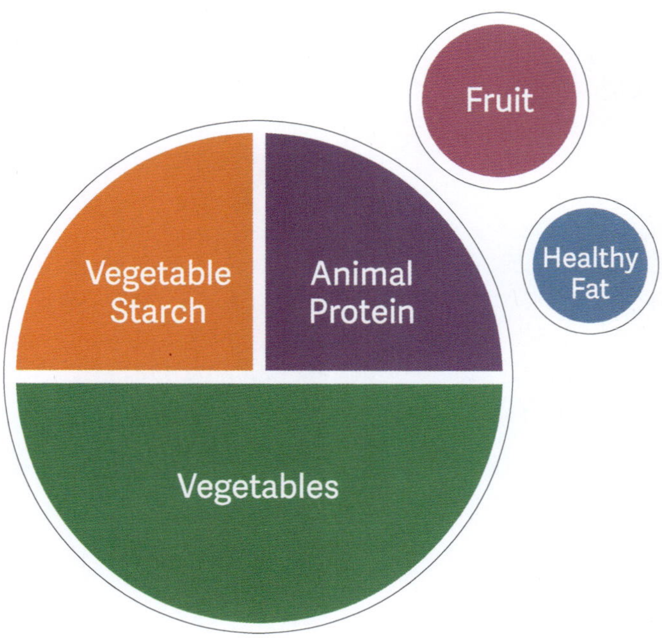

THE FOODS TO EMPHASISE

As I suggest to my clients, highlight everything on this list that you already eat or you like, or just don't eat very often. This is such a great mind trick and will show you just how many things you can eat during the elimination phase, perhaps you will even return to old favourite foods from your childhood you got out of the habit of eating or believed they were "unhealthy". This can be very comforting if you start to feel your food choices are restricted.

All the recipes in Part 3 are built from this list and I know you will end up with some new favourites which will become staple meals in your family for years to come. For example, you'll never use instant gravy ever again when you've tasted homemade gravy and realise how easy it is to make.

As a quick and easy summary, the AIP diet emphasises these foods, in order of priority:

1. Organ meats – such as liver, kidney and bone broth
2. Seafood – especially oily fish
3. Vegetables – especially green leafy vegetables and sea vegetables
4. Other meats – beef, lamb, pork and poultry
5. Starchy vegetables – root vegetables and squashes
6. Herbs and spices known for their anti-inflammatory properties – such as garlic, turmeric, ginger and thyme
7. Fruits
8. Healthy fats in small quantities – such as coconut oil, duck fat, goose fat, lard, avocado oil and olive oil

Animal Protein

Meats & organ meats
Antelope
Beef
Bone Broth
Goat
Heart
Horse
Lamb
Liver
Kidney
Pork
Rabbit
Veal
Venison

Poultry
Chicken
Duck
Goose
Guinea fowl
Ostrich
Pheasant
Quail
Turkey

Seafood
Anchovy
Bass
Clams
Cod
Crab
Eel
Haddock
Hake
Halibut
Herring
Lobster
Mackerel
Monkfish
Mussels
Octopus
Oysters
Prawns
Salmon
Sardine
Scallops
Shrimp
Snapper
Sole
Squid (calamari)
Swordfish
Tilapia
Trout
Tuna and all others

Starchy Vegetables

Arrowroot
Bamboo shoot
Beetroot
Breadfruit
Carrot
Cassava
Celeriac
Ginger
Horseradish
Jerusalem artichoke
Jicama (Mexican turnip)
Kohlrabi (German turnip)
Lotus root
Parsnip
Radish
Swede
Sweet potato (orange and white)
Taro
Tigernut
Turnip
Wasabi
Water chestnut
Yam

Non-Starchy Vegetables

Leafy vegetables
Beetroot greens
Brussels sprouts
Cabbage
(red, white & green)
Carrot greens
Celery
Chicory
Collard greens
Cress
Dandelion greens
Endive
Kale (many varieties)
Lettuce
(many varieties)
Mustard greens
Napa
(Chinese cabbage)
Radicchio
Rocket (arugula)
Spinach
Swiss chard
Turnip greens
Watercress

Other vegetables
Artichoke
Asparagus
Broccoli
Caper
Cauliflower
Edible flowers
Fennel bulb
Rhubarb (stems only)

Onion-family vegetables
Chive
Garlic
Leek
Onion
Shallot
Spring onions

Sea vegetables
Arame
Dulse
Kombu
Nor
Wakame

Vegetable-like fruits
Avocado
Bitter melon
Courgette (zucchini)
Cucumber
Okra
Olives
Plantain
Pumpkin
Squash (all varieties)
Winter melon

Fruits

Berries
Blackberry
Blueberry
Cranberry
Currant
Elderberry
Gooseberry
Grape
Loganberry
Raspberry
Strawberry

Tropical fruits
Banana
Coconut
Date
Dragonfruit
Durian
Fig
Guava
Jackfruit
Kiwi
Lychee
Mango
Mangosteen
Papaya
Passion fruit
Pawpaw
Persimmon
Pineapple
Pomegranate
Rambutan
Star fruit
Tamarind

Citrus-family fruits
Blood orange
Clementine
Grapefruit
Kaffir lime
Lemon
Lime
Mandarin
Meyer lemon
Orange
Pomelo
Satsuma
Tangerine
Yuzu

Rosaceae-family fruits
Apple
Apricot
Cherry
Nectarine
Peach
Pear
Plum
Quince
Rosehip

Melons
Cantaloupe
Galia
Honeydew
Horned melon
Persian melon
Watermelon

Healthy Fats

Animal fats
Bacon fat
Duck fat
Goose fat
Lard
Pan drippings
Tallow (rendered fat from beef, lamb or mutton)

Plant fats
Avocado oil (cold-pressed)
Coconut oil
Olive oil (cold-pressed)
Palm oil
Palm shortening

Other Pantry Staples

Edible fungi/mushrooms
Chanterelle
Cremini
Morel
Oyster
Porcini
Portobello
Shiitake
Truffle

Probiotic foods
Coconut yogurt
Fermented meat or fish
Fermented vegetables
Kimchi
Kombucha
Pickles
Sauerkraut
Water kefir

Sweeteners
Coconut sugar
Honey
Maple syrup

In small amounts

Leaf, flower, root, and bark spices
Basil leaf
Bay leaf
Chamomile
Chervil
Chives
Cinnamon
Cloves
Coriander leaf (cilantro)
Curry leaf
Dill
Fennel leaf
Fenugreek leaf
Garlic
Ginger
Horseradish (root)
Kaffir lime leaf
Lavender
Lemongrass
Mace
Marjoram
Onion powder
Oregano
Parsley
Peppermint
Rosemary
Saffron
Sage leaf
Salt
Spearmint
Tarragon
Thyme
Truffles
Turmeric

Other flavourings
Amchur, amchoor or aamchur powder (green mango powder)
Anchovies
Anchovy paste
Apple cider vinegar
Balsamic vinegar
Capers
Carob powder
Coconut aminos (a soy sauce substitute)
Coconut concentrate
Coconut milk
Coconut water vinegar
Fish sauce
Fruit and vegetable juice (in moderation)
Organic jams and chutneys
Red wine vinegar
Truffle oil (made with olive oil)
Vanilla
White wine vinegar

Food grade essential oils from spices (e.g. star anise, coriander seed, black pepper, cumin)

(always check for other ingredients when buying anything readymade)

A Note on Food Allergies and Intolerances

If you have any known food intolerances and allergies you will continue to avoid these foods, even if they are here on the AIP-approved list.

Try not to stick to the same few foods you like. Approach this as an opportunity to explore and experiment with new foods so your diet is diverse and varied.

Spotlight on Offal

In terms of your health, eating every part of an animal ensures you are eating the most nutrient dense diet. It will provide all the key amino acids that may be lacking if you eat either, predominantly muscle-meat or vegetarian sources of protein.

Organ meat is somewhat out of fashion and yet it's some of the most nutrient-rich (and most inexpensive) parts of the animal.

The word "offal" may not exactly whet your appetite and set your mouth watering, but it simply refers to edible parts of an animal that are not muscles: liver, kidney, skin, tongue, fat trimmings, blood and some bones for example.

Organ meats are nutritional power-houses with concentrated amounts of many of the vitamins and minerals which are frequently lacking in people with autoimmune and other chronic diseases, such as Vitamin A, all the Bs, but particularly B12, D and K and the minerals copper, iron, magnesium, selenium and zinc to name just a few.

As a minimum, aim to eat 4 meals per week containing offal to have a rapid, positive impact on the nutrient deficiencies common in autoimmune disease. As always, when it comes to good nutrition, aim for variety—liver, kidney, heart, poultry skin, bone broth from different animals is ideal. Sourcing your nutrients directly from your food will always be a better option than taking supplements. Supplements should be exactly that—supplemental—additional nutrition on top of an already nutrient-rich diet as needed for specific healing. You can never supplement your way out of a nutrient-poor diet.

As well as all the vitamins and minerals, offal tends to be higher in collagen than regular muscle meat and offal which contains a lot of connective tissue, such as skin and bones, are excellent sources of collagen. Collagen is quite the fashionable supplement these days, but it is possible to obtain it from your diet and reap the numerous additional nutritional benefits at the same time.

So, why is it so important to eat more collagen?

Glycine is the key amino acid found in collagen which makes up your connective tissue, literally the structure that holds you together—it's in everything from your skin, joint cartilage, tendons, the casing of your organs, muscles and blood vessels. Many autoimmune diseases feature degeneration in these very structures and a diet lacking in glycine means it's very difficult for the body to repair the damage. Eating these structures from other animals enhances your ability to build these structures in yourself.

You can think of it this way: if the roof on your home has a major leak but you don't have any roof tiles, you can of course patch the hole with some other bits and bobs you have lying around but it won't be as effective or as long-lasting as new roof tiles would be.

The same goes for physical damage in the body—your body will make glycine for repairing damaged tissue when your diet does not provide it in sufficient amounts, however it is not very efficient. Research seems to suggest the body cannot produce enough to keep up with the demands of a chronically ill body when dietary sources are low.

Eating glycine-rich foods will make a huge impact on your body's ability to heal the tissue damage caused by your autoimmune disease, including damage to the gut lining, blood vessels, skin and joints.

Bone Broth

If the idea of bringing more offal into your diet doesn't thrill you I recommend you begin with bone broth and work up to liver and other organs from there.

Bone broth is made from boiling the bones, joints and skin of any animal, in water for 24–48 hours. I add vegetables and herbs for flavour and the resulting liquid is rich in vitamins, minerals, calcium, magnesium, phosphorus and of course—glycine! It is the easiest way to increase your glycine intake and provide your body with the raw materials it needs to repair damage AND at the same time support your immune system.

Bone broth provides the additional benefit of healing the gut and reducing intestinal permeability. You will also reduce many of your gut symptoms and give your immune system a rest from being constantly triggered by food and pathogens passing across the vital gut barrier.

You can consume your bone broth in many ways:

- As a warm drink
- As a breakfast broth with added chicken, fresh herbs, ginger, spring onion and sauerkraut
- As "stock" in soups, stews and casseroles
- In gravy
- To poach meats and vegetables, Korean-style

Get creative and use bone broth wherever you would normally use water and you can easily consume it for the minimum 4 meals per week and beyond.

Liver

The liver of most animals is a highly nutritious food but they vary somewhat in nutrient content and flavour. Many people begin their liver journey with chicken livers; mild and small they are a great place to start.

My favourites in terms of texture and flavour are lamb's liver and calves' liver. Beef liver in particular is a nutritional superstar—meaning more goodness per mouthful than any other variety.

So, why is liver so good?

The standard western diet is lacking in many vitamins, minerals and essential fatty acids and is known to have a profound negative impact on immune function, resistance to infection and autoimmunity. A lack of dietary nutrients, and lack of fibre, combined with too many carbohydrates and refined seed oils have been strongly linked with the onset and progression of autoimmune disease.

Our reliance on foods which are not nutritionally dense, such as grains and dairy, crowd out the nutrient dense foods which include vegetables, fish, offal and grass-fed meat. As a result, we are severely lacking in the micronutrients which support robust health.

Liver is one of the top nutrient dense foods, high in the very vitamins and minerals which are severely lacking in people with autoimmunity and compromised immune function. These include the fat soluble Vitamin A (liver is one of THE best sources), Vitamin D (interestingly, studies have linked low Vitamin D levels with consumption of wheat bran) and Vitamin K. If you consume a very low fat diet you may well be deficient in these fat soluble vitamins.

Liver is also high in all the B vitamins especially Vitamin B12 (which is found only in animal food sources), copper, magnesium and iron in a form which is easily absorbed and used by the body. It is rich in selenium (required for thyroid function) and zinc which is a critical mineral for the immune system.

With research now showing so many vitamin and mineral deficiencies related to specific autoimmune diseases, it is critical to eat a diet rich in nutrient density and variety. No supplement is going to out-perform a varied, whole food diet and it's time to get happy with being in the kitchen more.

Eating 3–4 servings of offal a week, all varieties but particularly liver is one of the best ways to get the most nutrients per mouthful of food.

If you are serious about healing from autoimmune disease, then not liking liver is not an excuse to not consume it. If you really cannot stomach the thought of eating it here are a few hacks you can try:

- Grind it up in a food processor and add to minced beef in increasing ratios, starting with just a spoonful and moving towards 50:50
- Cut it up into pill-sized pieces (maybe ask someone to do this for you if you don't like the texture). Freeze the "pills" and then take a handful of "pills" with water every day—a better version of a multi-supplement and cheaper too!
- Start with pate rather than a whole piece of liver on a plate

Check out our four liver recipes in Part 3 to get you started, especially if this is a brand new food for you.

You may not like liver at the start but many of my clients have not only grown to enjoy it, they start to crave it!

I had one extreme situation working with a lovely client, Dawn. She had a strong dislike of liver because it had been used as a punishment food when she was a child. It was a very strong negative association, but Dawn was determined to be free from it and start nourishing herself in the best way possible. We worked on reframing her story around liver and she now loves it and eats it several times a week.

So you see, no matter how strongly you dislike something, your relationships with food and your limiting stories can change. (If my mum is reading this, she will now be on my case to reframe my own dislike story that I have around brussel sprouts!!)

FOODS TO AVOID

For a period of at least 30 days you will be avoiding the following foods because of their negative impact on the gut and inflammation. This may require longer for some people until symptoms have reduced significantly, 90 days is not uncommon.

You might be surprised to see many seemingly "healthy" foods on the list. As I have said already, whilst many foods, such as nuts and seeds, have a lot of nutritional content, they also contain high levels of some problematic compounds such as anti-nutrients which can work against digestion, especially in an already aggravated gut. So, you eliminate these for a period of time but they will be some of the first foods you reintroduce once the gut is healed, because of their high nutrient content. (See Appendix 2 for more on why these foods are removed).

As a quick and easy summary, we will avoid the following:

1. All grains and their products
2. All dairy products
3. All processed & packaged foods and food additives
4. All legumes (beans and peas)
5. All seeds and their products
6. All nuts and their products
7. All processed vegetable oils
8. All nightshade vegetables
9. All added sugar (with the exception of small amounts of coconut sugar, honey and maple syrup)
10. All alcohol

Excluded Foods

Grains
Barley
Bulgar
Corn
Durum
Kamut
Millet
Oats
Rice
Rye
Spelt
Wheat (all varieties, including einkorn and semolina)
Wild rice

Pseudo-Grains
Amaranth
Buckwheat
Chia
Quinoa

Dairy
Butter
Buttermilk
Butter oil
Cheese
Cottage cheese
Cream
Cream cheese
Curds
Dairy-protein isolates
Ghee
Heavy cream
Ice cream
Kefir
Milk
Sour cream
Whey
Whey-protein isolate
Whipping cream
Yogurt

Processed vegetable oils
Canola oil (rapeseed oil)
Corn oil
Cottonseed oil
Grapeseed oil
Palm kernel oil
Palm olein
Peanut oil
Safflower oil
Sunflower oil
Soybean oil
Vegetable oil

Excluded Foods (continued...)

Legumes (beans & peas)
Adzuki beans
Black beans
Black-eyed peas
Broad beans
Butter beans
Cannellini beans
Chickpeas
Great Northern beans
Green beans
Italian beans
Kidney beans
Lentils
Lima beans
Mange tout
Mung beans
Navy beans
Pinto beans
Peanuts
Peas
Runner beans
Split peas
Sugar snap peas
Soybeans (including edamame, tofu, tempeh, other soy products, and soy isolates, such as soy lecithin)

Nuts and nut oils
Almonds
Brazil nuts
Cashews
Chestnuts
Hazelnuts
Macadamia nuts
Pecans
Pine nuts
Pistachios
Walnuts

(Coconut is okay because it is not a nut)

Seeds and seed oils
Chia
Chocolate
Cocoa and cacao
Coffee
Flax
Hemp
Poppy
Pumpkin
Sesame
Sunflower

or any flavours, flours, butters, oils, or other products derived from nuts and seeds

Nightshades
Aubergine (eggplant)
Bell peppers (all colours)
Cayenne peppers
Cape gooseberries
Chili peppers
Goji berries
Paprika
Pimentos
Tamarillos
Tobacco
Tomatillos
Tomatoes
White potatoes (sweet potatoes are okay)

And all spices derived from these

Spices derived from seeds
Allspice
Anise
Black caraway
Black cumin
Black pepper
Cardamom
Celery seed
Coriander
Cumin
Dill seed
Fennel seed
Fenugreek
Juniper
Mustard
Nutmeg
Poppy

Food grade essential oils of spices are fine and make great alternatives.

Other Items
All alcohol
All eggs
All added sugar
All artificial sweeteners
Fake meat (vegetable textured protein and hydrolysed vegetable protein)

A little maple syrup, coconut sugar or raw honey is fine.

It looks a lot and I know there will be some favourites on this list you are going to miss. Remember why you are doing this: to eliminate SYMPTOMS—and it isn't going to be forever.

A Note about Processed Foods

Most convenience foods are chemical junk, even those with deceptively enticing labelling, such as "organic", "vegan" and "gluten-free". Turn to the ingredients label and you'll see a list of words you probably can't pronounce and foods you wouldn't be able to grow in your garden.

We are being encouraged more and more that convenience foods can be nutritious and "healthy" but nine times out of ten it's just not true. Home cooking, using whole foods in their natural state for most of your meals is the only way to ensure you are eating real food, nutrient dense food and healing foods. I'll talk more about this in Part 2.

If you can exclude all pre-packaged and processed food for the next 30 days you will go a long way to healing your gut, taming your inflammation and reducing your symptoms. Who knows how many additives our bodies are struggling to cope with? In Part 2, I will help you trouble-shoot the transition from convenience to nourishment with some of my top time-saving tips.

If you do still need to pick up some minimally-processed foods, such as tinned coconut milk, bacon and the like, become a reader of labels. Yes, I am sorry to say that a trip to the supermarket or your online shop may feel like a trip to the library for a while until you get to know the AIP-compliant brands for your favourite items.

One way I like to look at packaged food is this: if you couldn't grow it, catch it or make it yourself, don't eat it.

In the following list you will see some of the common additives that we don't want to be ingesting during the elimination phase (and rarely after that). As you'll see, what we are being encouraged to eat seems more like a chemistry set rather than food.

Before you throw your hands up in despair, let me give you two pieces of advice:

1. Go back to the Allowed Foods at the start of this chapter and revisit all the great foods you can have! There is a reason I made that section colourful—to appeal to your senses and draw you back again and again.
2. Don't stress if you inadvertently eat something that technically isn't allowed. It's okay, it happens to all of us. Beating yourself up, feeling like a failure and all the negative self-talk which comes with that, will do more to make your symptoms worse than a little maltodextrin (added sugar). Sometimes eating out or visiting friends can leave our choices slim, so choose the least offending option and enjoy the good company. I'll talk more on this in Part 2, overcoming the five main obstacles for an easy AIP transition.

Here are some of the food additives we want to avoid:

Processed food chemicals
Acrylamides
Artificial food colour
Artificial and natural flavours
Autolyzed protein
Brominated vegetable oil
Emulsifiers (carrageenan, cellulose gum, guar gum, lecithin, xanthan gum)
Hydrolysed vegetable protein (fake meat)
Monosodium glutamate
Nitrates or nitrites (naturally occurring are okay)
Olestra
Phosphoric acid
Propylene glycol
Textured vegetable protein (also fake meat)
Trans fats (partially hydrogenated vegetable oil, hydrogenated oil)
Yeast extract

and any ingredient with an unrecognised chemical name!

Sugar alcohols
Erythritol
Mannitol
Sorbitol
Xylitol

(Naturally occurring sugar alcohols found in whole foods like fruit are okay)

Artificial sweeteners
Acesulfame potassium
Aspartame
Neotame
Saccharin
Stevia
Sucralose

Added sugars
Agave and agave nectar
Barley malt and barley malt syrup
Beet sugar
Brown rice syrup
Brown sugar
Cane crystal
Cane juice
Cane sugar
Caramel
Corn sweetener
Corn syrup and corn syrup solids
Crystalline fructose
Date sugar
Demerara sugar
Dextrin
Dextrose
Diastatic malt
Evaporated cane juice
Fructose (natural in whole fruit is okay)
Fruit juice (used as an additive)
Fruit juice concentrate
Galactose
Glucose and glucose solids
Golden syrup
High-fructose corn syrup
Invert sugar
Inulin
Jaggery
Lactose
Malt syrup
Maltodextrin
Maltose
Monk fruit
Muscovado sugar
Palm sugar
Panela
Panocha
Raw cane sugar
Raw sugar
Refined sugar
Rice bran syrup
Rice syrup
Saccharose
Sorghum syrup
Sucanat
Sucrose
Syrup
Treacle
Turbinado sugar
Yacon syrup

It's all sugar folks! Leave it out.

CHAPTER 5

The Reintroduction Phase

The Elimination/Repair Phase is not supposed to be your long-term eating plan. That said, the vast majority of my clients end up saying to me "I feel so good eating this way, I don't want to reintroduce anything—except maybe coffee!"

There are some important reasons why you will want to reintroduce foods, and some less important ones too:

More Variety

With the right focus and attention, the elimination phase of the AIP diet can be very diverse and full of flavour but it's not uncommon for me to hear people say "I am getting a little bored of sweet potato" or "it would be nice to have eggs for breakfast sometimes".

Once your gut has healed, if a food is easily tolerated by your body, then there is no reason to exclude it, especially foods you really enjoy.

More Nutrient Density

Nutrient density is not just for the elimination phase—it's for life! From now onwards you want to be giving your body everything it needs to function optimally, so you feel great, have plenty of energy and joy for life.

Some of the foods we eliminate because they contain some gut-irritating compounds and anti-nutrients, still have a lot of valuable nutrition, especially eggs, nuts, seeds and legumes. Once again, so long as the gut has healed and these foods are well tolerated there is no need to exclude them long term.

More Flavour Variety

Many people miss the freedom of using all the spices they love. I certainly couldn't wait for some curries and chilis now and again. With the exception of chili (a nightshade), spices are the category of food least likely to cause problems and so it's one of the first food groups you can bring back in. Not only do spices add flavour, many of them have natural healing properties too and, once the gut is healed, including them in the diet can actually accelerate your healing process.

An Easier Social Life

Navigating a social life whilst following the AIP elimination phase can be challenging and I'll be talking about top tips for this in Part 2. When you know that it's only for a short period of time it makes it easier. Once you have gone through the reintroduction phase, you know which foods your body can handle from time to time and this can take away any anxiety around eating in restaurants and with friends.

Even if you choose not to eat certain foods at home anymore, knowing your body can tolerate certain foods occasionally means eating out is not only easier but it can also become a real treat. I rarely eat rice at home but enjoy having it at my favourite Thai restaurant and because I don't have it all the time, it makes it extra special when I do.

Avoiding Orthorexia Nervosa

No doubt you will have heard about eating disorders such as anorexia nervosa but did you know there is another recognised eating disorder called orthorexia nervosa?

Unlike eating disorders that revolve around the quantity of food, orthorexia is an unhealthy obsession around the quality of food. By loosening the control around the diet and allowing tolerated foods back in, we can ensure that we have a clear and healthy relationship with food.

A small number of foods will definitely be off the menu because they immediately bring on symptoms you don't want in your life anymore. These you can easily avoid by planning ahead, speaking with the restaurant staff and choosing something else on the menu. However, you don't want to create an unhealthy obsession around food or an exaggerated aversion to food.

Remember that whole food is nourishment and not to be feared or demonised.

A Note About Quantity

Food intolerances, allergies and their symptoms vary from person to person. What is easy to reintroduce for one person is an absolute no-no for someone else. Then there is a grey area around how much or how often a certain food is eaten.

Personally, I avoid gluten and anything that may contain it because I have an immediate reaction to it. Before I have even finished my meal, I have a bloated and uncomfortable belly and for several days after I will experience fatigue, brain fog and grumpiness. For me, it's just not worth it, as it negatively impacts my life for days.

On the other hand, rice I can tolerate once or twice per week with no problem. However, if it becomes something I eat every day (which can easily happen when travelling through Asia for example) then I start to get a low-grade fatigue and general fogginess. In cases like this it can be hard to pinpoint the cause of those feelings. By simply reflecting on my diet over the previous week and looking at how many "non-compliant" foods I have been indulging in, the links become clearer. Some foods have a tipping point beyond which you start to feel unwell but staying below it, is absolutely fine. Every person is unique and it takes time and inquisitiveness to figure the links out sometimes.

Approach the reintroduction phase as if you are Sherlock Holmes and become a detective. Document your results, remain curious, patient and neutral as you explore each new food.

Just because a food is not well tolerated when you try it for the first time, doesn't mean that food can never be eaten again. As the body continues to heal with your nutrient-rich diet, sensitivities can diminish. After a few months you can experiment with that food again and you may find the body now accepts it in small amounts.

How to Reintroduce New Foods

You want to reintroduce foods in a logical and systematic way if we are to glean the most information from the process. Introducing foods too quickly, too many at a time or as complex foods can be really confusing.

An example of a complex food would be chocolate cake. To try this means you are potentially reintroducing dairy, eggs, wheat flour, sugar and chocolate all at once. If you react to the chocolate cake, it's hard to know which was the problem ingredient? You have no way of knowing. By introducing each element one at a time you might discover you only have a problem with wheat flour. This is great news because you can easily find a recipe for wheat-free chocolate cake and continue to enjoy this sweet treat. Slow and steady really is the best way, otherwise you just wasted four weeks (or more) of eating compliantly to gain no information about your trigger foods moving forward.

Foods are reintroduced in order. You start with the foods least likely to cause a reaction and move towards those more likely to cause symptoms.

Top Tip: go through the list on the following pages and highlight every food you want to reintroduce. For example, if you never eat ghee then don't reintroduce it, simply focus on the foods you do want to eat again.

If you have a known allergy to a food such as eggs or peanuts you are not going to reintroduce these.

And if you have been avoiding additional foods, normally allowed on AIP, perhaps under the guidance of a nutritionist, you will **start your reintroductions with these** and then move to stage 1 foods.

Once you have your list it's time to start. It's a good idea to try the new foods at home. Since you have been avoiding these foods for several weeks, reactions can be very apparent and sometimes surprisingly fast—you don't want to be caught out. Begin with stage 1 reintroductions and slowly move up through the stages and take your time. Introduce new foods on a day when you feel reasonably well and not highly stressed, for the clearest feedback.

How to Test a New Food

- Select a food to reintroduce
- Start with half a teaspoon* or less and wait 15 minutes
  If there are reactions, stop and see instructions below~
- If there are no reactions, eat another full teaspoon and wait 15 more minutes
  If there are reactions, stop and see instructions below~
- If there are no reactions, eat one-and-a-half teaspoons and wait 2–3 hours
  If there are reactions, stop and see instructions below~
- If there are no reactions, eat a normal portion of the food and wait 3–7 days.

Do not reintroduce any other foods and track reactions during this time. If there are no reactions, that food can be brought back into your diet and you can begin another reintroduction.

* If introducing a spice or other item you normally only have in very small quantities—start with a little on the tip of the tongue, build up to half the amount you would consume in a dish. Then prepare a dish with the usual amount and consume that as normal.

~ If you have a reaction at any point in this process, stop and do not include this food in your diet at this time. Depending on the severity of your reaction, go back to the elimination phase until you reach the baseline of health that you had before you started reintroducing this food. This can take days or weeks to achieve but is important to do before you begin the process again with reintroducing a new food otherwise, it will be difficult to gauge positive or negative reactions to the next reintroduction attempts.

Symptoms to Look Out for During Reintroductions

As you introduce new foods, keep a symptom journal detailing which food you are testing and your symptoms for 3–7 days. The kinds of symptoms you may experience include:

- Changes in your sleep pattern
- New cravings – for sugar, caffeine, fat, salt
- Skin rashes and spots
- Changes to hair and nails
- Aches and pains – either usual ones felt more intensely, or brand new ones
- Any changes to digestion and bowel movements – including bloating, indigestion, diarrhoea, constipation
- Mood changes – mood swings, anxiety, depression, low tolerance to stress
- Fatigue – including afternoon energy dips
- Increased phlegm, congestion and sneezing
- Headaches
- Dizziness, light-headedness and brain fog
- Coughing and excessive throat clearing
- Itchiness
- An increase in your disease symptoms generally

That's quite a lot but don't add stress to the process by anticipating negative reactions. Your digestive and immune systems are aggravated by stress and this will make the process harder. Rest assured that you will be able to reintroduce many new foods to your diet. It can be a frustrating process so I encourage you to remain patient as much as you can.

Stage 1 Foods

Egg yolks (not the whites)

Legumes (beans with edible pods, and legume sprouts)
Green beans
Peas
Runner beans
Mangetout
Mungbean sprouts
Sugar snap peas

Fruit and berry-based spices
Allspice
Star anise
Caraway
Cardamom pod
Juniper
Pepper (from black, green, pink or white peppercorns)

Dairy (ideally from grass-fed sources)
Ghee

Seed-based spices
Anise seed
Black caraway
Black cumin
Celery seed
Coriander seed
Cumin seed
Dill seed
Fennel seed
Fenugreek
Mustard
Nutmeg

Nuts and seeds (oils only)
Macadamia
Sesame
Walnut

Nuts and seeds
Chocolate (dark not milk)
Cocoa, cacao
Coffee (occasional basis)

Stage 2 Foods

Nuts and seeds
Almonds
Brazil nuts
Cashews
Chestnuts
Coffee (daily basis)
Hazelnuts
Macadamia nuts
Pecans
Pine nuts
Pistachios
Walnuts
Chia
Flax
Hemp seeds
Poppy
Pumpkin seed
Sesame
Sunflower

and any other flavours, flours, butters, oils and other products derived from them

Egg whites (or whole eggs)

Dairy (ideally from grass-fed sources)
Butter
Butter oil

Alcohol (small quantities)
Gluten-free beer (8 oz. or less)
Gluten-free cider (8 oz. or less)
Wine (5 oz. or less)
Fortified wine (3 oz. or less)
Gluten-free spirits (1 oz. or less).

Stage 3 Foods

Nightshades (limited)
Bell peppers (aka sweet peppers)
Aubergine (eggplant)
Paprika
Potatoes (peeled)

Legumes
Chickpeas (aka garbanzo beans)
Lentils
Split peas

Dairy (ideally from grass-fed sources)
Buttermilk
Cheese
Cottage cheese
Cream
Cream cheese
Curds
Dairy-protein isolates
Heavy cream
Ice cream
Kefir
Milk
Sour cream
Whey
Whey-protein isolate
Whipping cream
Yogurt

Legumes and grains may be more well tolerated when soaked and sprouted

Stage 4 Foods

Nightshades or spices derived from nightshades
Cayenne peppers
Cape gooseberries
Goji berries
Hot peppers (chili peppers and chili-based spices
Pimentos
Potatoes (unpeeled)
Tamarillos
Tomatoes

Gluten-free grains and pseudo-grains
Amaranth
Buckwheat
Corn
Millet
Oats
Quinoa
Rice
Wild rice

Legumes
Adzuki beans
Black beans
Black-eyed peas
Broad beans (aka fava beans)
Butter beans
Cannellini beans
Great Northern beans
Italian beans
Kidney beans
Lima beans
Mung beans
Navy beans
Pinto beans
Peanuts
Soy

Alcohol (moderate quantities)
Gluten-free beer
Gluten-free cider
Wine
Fortified wine
Gluten-free spirits

CHAPTER 6

The Maintenance Phase

At the end of the Reintroduction Phase you will end up with a bespoke diet that is right for you at this point in time and may continue to evolve as your health continues to improve. This becomes Stage 4: the Maintenance Phase.

Many people find they eat mostly AIP-compliant ingredients with a few favourite reintroductions about 80% of the time, especially at home because they have simply cultivated the habit of cooking and eating this way. You will also be familiar with which of your favourite restaurants can accommodate you being gluten-free and that continues to be easy to navigate.

The remaining 20% of the time allows for a few indulgences and treats that you know you can tolerate well occasionally, such as special holidays, celebrations and socialising.

If you approached this diet as a lifestyle change rather than a quick fix then you are unlikely to return to a diet of fizzy drinks, processed food and white bread. If you do revert to that, your body will very quickly tell you it's not happy.

An Annual Clean-Up

Once you have established your bespoke plan, eating can feel pretty normal again, even if you remain entirely gluten-free and/or dairy-free. There are times though when things slip a bit and old habits re-establish themselves. I particularly find this happens when other life routines are thrown up in the air as well. This can happen around holidays, celebrations, house guests, vacations and even periods of illness.

It can be a good idea to make a pledge to yourself right from the start that at least once a year you will have a compliant period of 2–4 weeks to reset good habits before you get too far off track. If you have already been eating AIP 80% of the time anyway, it's not such a big change to return to it 100% for this short time. Once the clean-up period is complete you can bring those foods back in that you know your body tolerates well, but it is still a good idea to go somewhat slowly as you may realise that something isn't as well tolerated as you thought, especially if you have noticed any recent increase in symptoms prior to the doing the clean-up.

So that's the AIP diet—food and process—in a nutshell. In Part 2 I will be talking about the five biggest obstacles people commonly encounter and how to overcome them, so that your transition to better health with AIP is smooth and successful.

Read on!

PART 2

THE COMMON PITFALLS WITH AIP AND HOW TO AVOID THEM

CHAPTER 7

Eating Well Does Not Have to Take All Day

There is no doubt that we live in a time of convenience and immediate gratification. Everything is available, with next day delivery, in any colour, size and at any time you want.

We accept this as normal. Have you ever decided to shop elsewhere because an online store can't deliver for three days? We all have, I'm sure.

Convenience has really become our new normal when it comes to food as well. Everything is available "to go" and eating has become either a pitstop to refuel the tank or an invitation to overindulge and "treat" ourselves as a reward for surviving another day in our busy world, all available and within easy reach.

Our grandparent's generation was so unbelievably different and its not all that long ago. Food was made from scratch, by hand and much of it was grown in their own garden. Food took time to prepare and nourishment was honoured and respected. We ate together, we had rituals around food and we were connected to where our food came from as well as to the seasons which produced it.

My mum and dad often used to recount stories such as the first time they ever saw bananas in the UK after the war. These days bananas are so commonplace in our supermarkets we've perhaps started to think of them as local produce rather than tropical fruit.

As society changed and women, thankfully, enjoyed careers outside the home, home-cooking perhaps felt old-fashioned and out of touch with progress and the speed at which technology and industry was moving. It became 'the norm', fashionable and acceptable to eat convenience and processed foods.

There will always be a trade-off between convenience and nourishment and to eat well for great health you are going to have to get excited about being in the kitchen again. However, you do not need to be a slave to it and spend all day there. I am going to show you how you can cook delicious and nutritious meals AND save 10–15 hours in the kitchen each week.

I have three big time-saving tips for you.

Read on!

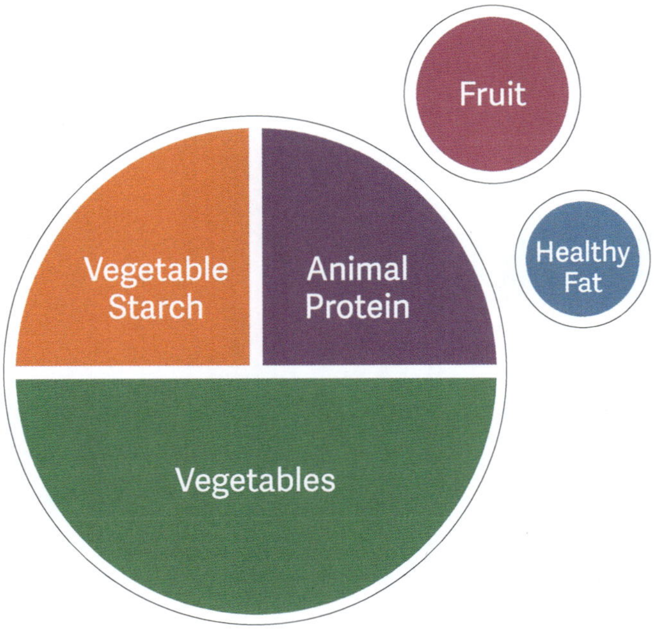

Keep It Simple!

Review the food plate again—remember that for at least two out of three meals each day, you ideally want an animal protein, a starch and vegetables. Start creating some tasty combinations from foods you already enjoy.

Review the colour coded lists in Chapter 2 to make easy selections from each category. Select a meat or fish, a starchy root and a selection of veggies. Throw in a little fruit and some healthy fats and you have created your first AIP-compliant meal.

This is such a great habit that everyone in the family can use to build a nutritionally balanced plate and a habit you can continue to use long into the future, without any brain ache.

An example might be roast chicken (animal protein), roasted sweet potatoes with parsnips (starchy roots) and steamed broccoli (vegetables). Easy!

It's important for nutrition and enjoyment, not to eat the same thing day in, day out since different foods contain different vitamins, minerals, essential fatty acids and phytonutrients. Work down the list of animal proteins so you don't always select chicken (which apart from a good source of protein, is quite nutrient-poor relative to other meats). Experiment with new roots that you may not have heard of—see our spotlights for more on some of these.

Select from the delicious recipes in Part 3 which are all AIP-compliant and can give you a place to start, keep your taste buds happy and inspire you when food starts to feel repetitive.

A good guideline is to have fish 3–5 meals per week, organ meat (which includes bone broth) at least four times per week and fill in the rest of your meals from the remainder of the list of proteins.

Make a Shopping List for the Week

This one may feel old fashioned but it's so effective.

Have you ever gotten home late from work, with a hungry family looking at you like characters from Oliver Twist, and you have no idea what to make for dinner? It's stressful, exhausting and more likely to lead to poor food choices: where you choose convenience over nourishment.

Never again!

By planning out your meals for an entire week and writing a shopping list, not only do you save time, but you also reduce stress at home and increase the likelihood of eating more nutritious foods every day. You may need to shop twice in the week, especially for fresh produce but you have your list prepared, so you only need to think about it once per week.

I already introduced you to this idea in The Preparation Phase but maintaining it as a weekly discipline is key to being successful and, more importantly, enjoying your AIP diet.

With Hashimoto's Thyroiditis, brain fog was a big part of my condition, along with mental fatigue. Add to that the feelings of hunger at the end of the day and I had no tolerance for thinking about meals in the evening.

By taking a leisurely couple of hours to plan your week ahead, at a time of day when your focus is at its best, is a game changer to making the AIP diet a success. Coupled with batch-cooking you can take all the indecision, stress and frustration out of meals. And of course, save time.

The reason I say to give yourself a few days to get all your ducks in a row at the start of the diet is to conserve your energy—both physical and mental as you move forward. But weekly meal planning can become a regular habit to support you back to healthy eating with no slip ups.

This is what I recommend:

- Take one day to plan all the meals for the week ahead and write out a shopping list. Take into account social activities, after school clubs, and potentially problematic days where free time will be in short supply
- The next day you shop for the items on your list and
- The third day you can get ahead of the game by batch cooking and preparing some foods in advance.

You can conserve even more energy if online food shopping is available in your area, especially for the heavy and mundane foods or even recruit family members to shop for you, which is much easier if you have a list.

I had one client who really got her teenage children involved. She challenged each of them to come up with an AIP-compliant meal for the whole family once a week, shop for it and cook it. It was a total success and as they became more involved, they learned about the importance of reading ingredient labels, eating a balanced plate and were really creative in their culinary creations.

It was eye-opening for the whole family to see just how much unpronounceable rubbish so many of our foods contain. We eat things habitually but rarely take the time to read the back of the packet.

Even just choosing two or three new recipes from this book each week will set the whole family on the road to eating more nutritional variety.

Be sure to read all of Part 2 before you plan out your meals for the week, so you don't fall into any of the other pitfalls. So, read on and come back here to make your shopping list when you have read all of Part 2!

Batch Cooking

This is the most unbelievable time-saver in the kitchen and something every busy person who wants to eat well can benefit from.

You can literally save hours this way. Think about it:

- If you are cooking a roast chicken and you know you want chicken later in the week, why not cook both chickens together, if your oven is big enough?
- If your recipe calls for half a chopped onion, chop the whole thing or even chop two and store in an airtight container for another recipe later in the week.

These are just 2 simple examples of time saving tips. If you are in the kitchen attending to one meal, in those quiet moments when you are waiting for something to come to the boil or finish grilling, prepare some chopped or grated veggies for a meal tomorrow.

I had one client who ended up treating this as something of a game. She would chop up all her veggies when she brought them back from the supermarket and store them all in glass containers in the fridge. Half the onions were diced, the other half sliced; cauliflower was grated and frozen, carrots sliced or grated and stored in water and so on. Check out the pre-chopped veggies in your local supermarket too. These are great for throwing together a quick soup—a bag of chopped vegetables, homemade bone broth and leftover chicken—a quick blitz with a hand blender and lunch is ready in 20 minutes. Even easier if you have a soup kettle.

Batch cooking, along with your meal plan for the week, is a way of getting ahead of the game and making your own, super healthy version of the ready meal, that you can freeze and just warm up on those days when you know you will be pressed for time. Dashing in late after taking your children to swimming lessons or football practice, is a prime time for the alluring convenience of a takeaway pizza to seem really appealing. Knowing you have your delicious leftover beef stew waiting for a quick warm through whilst you steam some broccoli will keep you from deviating to your phone to order in. And of course, you never know when you are going to have one of those out-of-the-blue days when fatigue just knocks you off your feet and you haven't got the energy for anything. Hello leftover soup!

When I make most meals, I try to make at least double, either to freeze for those busy days, or as a quick lunch or breakfast the next day. This way you are only preparing food once—saving time and mental effort. Get into the habit right from the start of making and using leftovers for tomorrow.

Here are a few of my top tips when it comes to batch cooking:

- Cook double quantities and use leftovers the next day or freeze and use on another day.
- Fill in your idle time when making one meal to prepare for tomorrow's meal—saving time tomorrow.
- Chop all veggies that you can in advance and store in airtight containers in the fridge or freezer (some will need to be in water to stop discolouration). This includes preparing onions, garlic and ginger that will become staples for your cooking.
- Make one or two salad dressings in advance and store in glass jars.
- Buy ready chopped veggies if your budget will stretch to it. They are often reduced when they are near their sell-by date, saving money as well as time.

- Make a batch of bone broth, strain, cool and refrigerate and then immediately top the pot of bones back up with water and cook for another 24 hours to make a batch to freeze. Most bones will give you two batches of broth.
- Bones store well in the freezer, so if you have plenty of bone broth already, don't throw away that chicken carcass. Store it in an airtight container or tin foil in the freezer to make broth another time when you have no bones to hand.
- Soup. That's a full sentence really. You can make one big pot of soup and store/freeze in portions that you can just grab and go for breakfast, lunch, dinner or a snack.

Here are my favourite things to cook in bulk because they store really well and taste great:

- Soup!
- Bone broth
- Stews and casseroles
- Meat patties
- Cabbage
- Riced cauliflower
- Condiments and salad dressings
- Coleslaw (only add the dressing as you are ready to eat it)
- Roasted meat
- Savoury mince

These tips are just the start, as you approach cooking with efficiency in mind, I am sure you will come up with some creative hacks of your own. Reframe home cooking as a priority but not something that must take all day, because it really doesn't have to.

CHAPTER 8

The Breakfast Dilemma

When someone looks at the list of foods to avoid, there is a moment of realisation that passes over their face—100% of the time. They look up from the list, look at me with a mild sense of horror and ask, "what on earth am I going to have for breakfast?"

The Western breakfast is the most boring, inflammation-promoting and repetitive meal of the day for most people. It comprises various combinations of wheat, milk, sugar, coffee and eggs... none of which are eaten during the elimination/repair phase. With the exception of eggs, which are a superfood, in my opinion, these ingredients provide a quick energy hit, followed by a crash, and contain almost no valuable nutrients.

Most people in the West eat from these 5 ingredients every single morning, some eat only one or two of these, leading to even less nutritional variety. Would you approach your evening meal this way? Eating the same thing, day in, day out? Probably not, so why do we do it for breakfast?

One of the quickest ways to bring more nutrients, more variety, more stable blood sugar and fewer cravings into your life is to change your relationship with breakfast. Mix it up, like you do for dinner.

We also need to reframe what breakfast is from "coffee and toast" to the first nutritious meal of the day, the meal that breaks our 12–14 hour night-time fast.

If something is delicious and healthy at noon or 6 pm, it's just as delicious and nutritious when eaten at 7 am. It requires a shift of mindset away from the one we adopted from our cultural conditioning. After all, one third of the world's population begin their day with soup, so why can't we?

For better energy levels throughout the day and fewer cravings in the afternoon I recommend moving more of your calorie intake to earlier in the day and ensuring there is protein at breakfast. I now eat a breakfast that is at least the same size as my evening meal. I have reduced my lunch in size and my energy remains consistent all day, every day—no after lunch slump and no food cravings. One additional benefit is that I have reached and maintained my ideal weight without calorie-counting.

Many people don't eat breakfast at all. They rely on coffee to get them going but this is just setting the body up for poor energy levels. Coffee gives the adrenal glands an artificial jump-start and when the inevitable crash follows, they find themselves reaching for either more coffee or something sweet (or both). If that sounds like you, I encourage you to start cultivating a breakfast habit. Start small and build up slowly.

So, what will you eat for breakfast?

Here are some of my favourites.

Leftovers

Literally, I make double the quantity of my meal in the evening and warm it up the next morning. I cannot imagine ever wanting toast or cereal in the morning now, I look at them and they have all the appeal of eating a cardboard box. Whereas, leftover beef stew with some wilted spinach thrown in is scrumptious...especially on cold mornings.

My favourite breakfast leftovers include wok-cooked cabbage or riced cauliflower, just reheated, casseroles, roast chicken, baked salmon, or roasted veggies. I pretty much eat yesterday's evening meal the next morning, quite happily.

Bone Broth

Bone broth is another favourite. I warm it up, throw in some chopped spring onions, a little fresh ginger, spinach and some cooked chicken if it's in the fridge for a satisfying and anti-inflammatory warm broth. Very healing for the gut, wonderful for your immune system, packed with nutrients and very satisfying on a cold morning.

Sweet Potato Rounds

These make a lovely addition to a cooked breakfast plate. Simply slice a sweet potato with skin on into 1 cm thick rounds. Rub in some olive oil and salt and bake in the oven at 200 degrees Celsius for 15–20 minutes whilst you prepare what to have them with or take a shower. You could just as easily do this with slices of butternut squash as well.

I like to pair my sweet potato rounds with meat patties that I quickly cook in a pan and finish the ensemble with half an avocado and some fresh, raw baby spinach.

Meat Patties

The basic template to make 6–8 patties (depending on how big you make them) is:

500g minced meat
2 TBSP finely chopped onion
A twist of salt
A sprinkle of herbs

I have not put exact amounts of herbs because I never measure them—just add to match your palette and cook a small one to test the flavour first. If making them for the first time start with a ½ teaspoon—you can always add more but you can't take it out if you over-do it.

Throw all the ingredients into a bowl and mix it thoroughly with your hands, squeezing together to encourage them to bind and to remove any excess water. Divide into six or eight balls and shape into patties (mini burgers).

Heat 1–2 tablespoons of coconut oil in a pan and cook both sides. It usually takes about 10 minutes to fully cook, depending on the heat of your pan. You can either cook them all up and save some for later in the fridge or freezer—just reheat to eat. I tend to just keep the uncooked patties in the fridge or freezer in greaseproof paper and cook fresh as needed.

My favourite combinations are:
Minced beef with thyme
Minced pork with sage or oregano
Minced chicken with tarragon
Minced ostrich (or venison) with rosemary

You can do anything, so don't be afraid to experiment.

Soup

When I was a university student and living on a shoestring, I would go to the local fruit and vegetable market at the end of the day on a Saturday and pick up anything left over that the sellers didn't want to take home again. I would literally fill two carrier bags with fresh vegetables, go home and turn it into a big pot of vegetable soup or stew. All for 50p per carrier bag. Ok, so that was more than 30 years ago, but even in today's money it would only be £2.50.

It was so inexpensive, packed with goodness and I always had something quick for breakfast or lunch.

If you make your vegetable soup with bone broth you are getting an amazing boost to your nutritional stores. You can add in anything left over, looking a bit sad in the fridge, some chopped chicken or bacon to get a little more protein in there. Compare that nutritionally with coffee and toast—there really is no comparison. One will build up your health and one will make you sick. Before you jump in and say but toast tastes better, it doesn't, it's just that you're used to it—it's a habit. Any habit can be changed and become your new normal.

If you love soup and think you'll be making a lot, consider investing in a soup kettle, which will cook and blend your soup in just 20 minutes, whilst you get on with other things.

I think soup is great to have, not just for breakfast but for those times when you want a hot lunch on the go (invest in a good thermos) or you are short on time and could easily fall prey to your old eating habits.

Coconut Yogurt with Fruit

Fruit is encouraged in moderation during the elimination phase. It's packed full of great nutrition and fibre but is also high in natural sugar. Fruit is a great way to get a sweet fix but do be mindful not to overload on the sugar, it should still make up only a small proportion of your daily diet.

If the thought of a savoury breakfast really puts you off, especially if you are new to eating anything in the morning, then try homemade coconut yogurt with fruit. In time, as your metabolism adjusts to receiving fuel in the morning, your body will start to feel hungry and you can alternate between a sweet and a savoury breakfast, eventually emphasising the savoury breakfast more often.

It is unbelievably easy to make your own coconut "yogurt":

Put a can of whole coconut milk (400ml) in the fridge for a few hours. Remove but do not shake. The solid coconut cream will have separated from the water. Scoop out the coconut cream and whip with a hand blender, adding a little of the coconut water if it is too thick.

It will take on a thick yogurt consistency. Add a drop or two of vanilla essence, some vanilla seeds, carob or cinnamon powder for variety. This also makes a delicious dessert as well, either as a yogurt, or add a couple of drops of vanilla essence (or a vanilla pod) and freeze to make an alternative vanilla ice cream.

Bacon

Arguably the best breakfast flavour, bacon is a great familiar addition to your morning meal. It's time to read ingredients labels however, since not all bacon is created equal. Many brands have added sugar, artificial flavours and preservatives. Compare what's available in your supermarket or online. Avoid those with the most ingredients and definitely those with added sugar. You can take a view on the additives. Strictly, they would be off-limits, but if symptoms are improving for you then you could probably tolerate bacon with a preservative or two, a few times per week.

If you find your symptoms are not improving, then it might be time to really hone in on these "micro-ingredients" and eliminate them completely.

I love to pair bacon with sweet potato rounds, baby spinach and avocado or with reheated, leftover red cabbage—yum!

Salmon, Mackerel and Trout

Many cultures have a breakfast fish option, such as kippers or smoked salmon so it's not too much of a stretch to consider adding fish to your first meal of the day.

The same issue applies as it does for bacon. You will need to read the ingredients, as many smoked options have a lot of artificial ingredients. If in doubt, simply cook an extra salmon fillet the night before and have one cold and flaked for breakfast with half an avocado and sweet potato rounds. Mackerel is a quick and easy option, available in most supermarkets.

Of course, you can always open a tin of sardines, mackerel or tuna as an option as well. Not only quick and nutritious but works within most budgets.

Salad

Salad is another food that many of us confine to a particular meal, like lunch for example. If you have travelled further afield and enjoyed an international buffet breakfast, no doubt you will have seen many people filling up their plate with salad.

It's worth embracing this attitude too. Having salad for breakfast is a great way to get more vegetables, especially leafy greens, into your daily diet. We have all heard that we should be eating five portions of fruit or vegetables a day (in fact it's more like 10 for optimal health) and by adding salad and vegetables, as well as a little fruit to your breakfast, you can tick off that target before you even leave the house.

CHAPTER 9

Flavour

Claire's Love of Flavour

I love food, I think I have said that already. So, when I embarked on the AIP elimination diet I was not prepared to settle for bland, repetitive food. I truly believe nutritious food can be and should be, delicious.

There are of course, many flavours off the menu for a while—things like chili and some spices but there are many ways to bring a large variety of flavour to your meals and who knows, you might explore some new ones that you discover that you really love.

I am a keen traveller and have lived in several countries. One of the best parts of travelling is trying new cuisine and as a keen cook (but not a trained chef), I also love to replicate these dishes at home, albeit with my own twist. So, turning familiar dishes into AIP versions was not that much of a challenge for me once I had become familiar with my new pantry.

I grew up in England in the 1970s and 80s not that long after food rationing ended. I remember years of trade union strikes and an economic recession during that time. The British, at least back then, were not known for their exciting or varied cuisine. My comfort food, though, is definitely rooted in the traditions of home from the 1970s. I mostly remember winter food since I was so busy out playing in the summer that mealtimes were the quickest of pit-stops before dashing outside again to enjoy the long, light summer evenings.

I love stews, casseroles, roast dinners with gravy, vegetables and for dessert—custard. They bring back feelings of being loved and feeling snug. My chores as a child were to make the gravy, custard and lay the table; traditions I still adhere to today.

I left home at 18 to attend university and that's where I had my first mind-blowing encounters with exotic food—spaghetti bolognaise, Chinese takeaway, Indian flavours and chili con carne. Not exotic by today's standards (or by Sue's upbringing as you'll read shortly) but for me it was an awakening for my palette and firmly established me as a lover of food and flavour... a trait I am happy to say I share with my husband who is an excellent, self-taught cook. I seem to have passed a love of food and flavour on to my son too, a great asset as he embarks on his adult life.

Over the years I have also lived in Arizona, South Africa and Thailand, adopting local tastes and techniques along the way, all of which I have brought to my AIP kitchen.

It really saddens me when I hear people say things like "AIP makes me feel good but the food is so boring and restrictive I couldn't do it for long". It does not have to be that way but, it has to be said: if you want your food to be both nutritious and delicious you are going to have to accept that it's down to you. As you begin to feel better and have more energy, get more comfortable and happy with being in the kitchen. Challenge yourself to try new foods and flavours and move away from convenience food.

Feeding yourself and creating flavour your taste buds will tingle for, is an act of self-love as well as self-nourishment. Digestion begins before any food has entered your digestive system. It begins with the senses—the aroma of food cooking, the sight of a beautifully prepared dish all kick-start the digestive system: our mouth starts to water and our tummy rumbles as the digestive juices begin to flow in anticipation of food arriving.

As we get older, it's common to produce less stomach acid and lower levels of digestive enzymes, making it harder for us to break down the food we eat. This is also associated with low thyroid function and Hashimotot's. Low stomach acid and digestive enzymes can cause digestive problems, leaky gut, an imbalance in our gut bacteria and even lead to poor absorption of nutrients. So, getting these key digestive enzymes flowing is really important, on so many levels.

I still love to plate food in a beautiful way, even if I am eating alone and I lay the table for every meal, sitting to enjoy the food and the break that mealtime affords us in our over-scheduled lives.

Creating food that smells good and looks beautiful, involves two of our five senses. We might also prepare food and eat it with our hands to bring alive the sense of touch. We awaken the senses of hearing and touch through the use of texture: crunchy food, squeaky food, crispy food and even slurping a hearty soup.

But of course, the key sense is taste, which brings us back to the topic of flavour.

I approach flavour in the same way I approach the whole AIP elimination phase. I focus on what I can have, use as much variation here as I can and mentally let go of what is excluded. Many favourite dishes can be easily made AIP-compliant, such that you need never go back to the old ways of preparing them. Other dishes require a little more creativity and Part 3 will give you some tried and tested versions to begin with so you don't have to reinvent the wheel. Some other dishes we may just have to let go of for a while, such as a hot curry or chili con carne but not necessarily forever.

My top list of flavours are:

- Lemongrass
- Ginger
- Turmeric
- Kaffir lime leaves
- Grated horseradish for when you need a spicy kick
- Wasabi – go for the powder since the prepared wasabi often has other ingredients included which are not AIP-compliant
- Radish
- Onion
- Garlic
- All the herbs – fresh and dried (it's worth establishing a fresh herb box in the garden or on a large windowsill so you always have fresh on hand)
- Coconut aminos
- Apple cider vinegar
- Balsamic vinegar
- Anchovies
- Tamarind
- Lemons, limes and oranges – juice and rind
- Food grade essential oils in place of non-compliant spices such as black pepper, star anise, cumin and coriander seed

To thicken sauces, soups and gravies I use arrowroot powder.

Spotlight on Arrowroot Powder

In my pre-AIP days, I would usually thicken sauces with wheat flour or cornflour, both of which are grains and excluded during the elimination phase. A terrific substitute is arrowroot powder. Arrowroot is a tuber, a little like a sweet potato, native to Indonesia and can be ground into a powder.

It has additional benefits since it is high in protein and several key minerals such as iron and potassium and is one of the best sources of folate (Vitamin B9), low levels of which are associated with an increased risk of chronic disease.

Gravy is one of my favourite foods and a diet without it would be tragic indeed. I can honestly say that the recipe for my husband Neil's gravy, included in Part 3 is the best gravy I have ever had and is totally AIP-compliant. Your non-AIP family members will love it!

Spotlight on Coconut Aminos

I had never heard of coconut aminos before I embarked on my AIP transition and was really surprised I could actually find it in the supermarket in our small, rural South African town.

Before I tell you what it is, let me tell you what we use it for. Often, we add condiments to dishes to deepen the flavour and add complexity for the taste buds. Traditionally in the East soy sauce is used for this; in the West we might select yeast extract, Marmite or Worcestershire sauce.

Unfortunately:

- Soy is excluded and soy sauce usually also contains wheat
- Yeast extract and Marmite come from wheat or barley—both excluded
- Worcestershire sauce also contains wheat and other excluded ingredients

So how do we deepen the flavour of our AIP dishes?

Say hello to coconut aminos! It's a dark-coloured sauce which tastes similar to soy sauce. Instead of being made from soy, however, coconut aminos is obtained from the sap of the coconut flowers (not the coconuts). After extraction, the sap is stored and aged and during this time, it ferments due to the natural sugars present within it. The final result tastes savoury and not at all like coconut and is totally safe to use when doing the AIP elimination phase.

There are extra bonuses too, it's:

- low in salt (unlike soy sauce)
- high in amino acids (protein building blocks) as the name suggests
- and since it is fermented, it is a probiotic food helping you to maintain a healthy gut microbiome, which is critical for good mental and physical health

Coconut aminos is another ingredient we have carried on using instead of soy or Worcestershire sauce as it does the job so well and is soy, gluten and additive free.

Food Grade Essential Oils

Many favourite spices are excluded during the elimination phase due to the presence of anti-nutrients. These are naturally occurring plant compounds a plant uses to resist being digested. They are commonly found in seeds, legumes and grains. When an animal eats a seed for example, the seed wants to pass through the digestive tract of the animal undigested so it can be deposited in fertile soil and grow into a new plant.

Anti-nutrients, in small amounts, are not normally a problem in a healthy individual but can become problematic if a diet is based largely on grains and legumes or if the gut has become too permeable as we commonly find in autoimmune disease.

Spices from these high anti-nutrient foods are excluded whilst the gut heals.

One way around this exclusion is to substitute the spice with the essential oil. The anti-nutrients tend to be in the water-soluble portion of the food. Essential oils are drawn out of plants via steam distillation or cold pressing and only contain volatile fat-soluble compounds, leaving the anti-nutrients behind.

Essential oils are commonly used in the food industry as flavouring. So, if you really miss your favourite spices you can substitute with the essential oil. A couple of cautions:

1. Ensure the brand you select is safe for ingestion since most essential oils are actually 100% synthetic or a mixture of pure oil with synthetic copies, despite what it says on the label. There is very little regulation of the essential oil industry and most are at best, fragrance and not appropriate to ingest.

2. Essential oils are very, very concentrated. If the recipe calls for 1 teaspoon of dried spice, you only need one drop, maximum, of the essential oil.

One more benefit of using essential oils is less waste. I am forever finding old packets of limp, slimy herbs at the bottom of the fridge which have gone off before I had a chance to use them up. Also, when travelling or eating out, oils such as citrus, black pepper and coriander are handy to have in your handbag to add to restaurant food to make it more interesting.

I also love to add essential oils to my drinking water (always in a glass bottle—not plastic) to make water more interesting and for their various health benefits.

The human race has been making use of the chemistry found in plants for thousands of years as flavouring, preservatives and natural and effective medicine.

Some of my favourite oils to add to water are all the citrus oils, ginger, peppermint and spearmint. It makes sure I remain properly hydrated and you can use warm water too for a kind of "tea" or carbonated water for a spritzer.

When it's time to re-introduce some seeds, legumes and grains you can remove much of the anti-nutrient content by using traditional preparation methods such as soaking in water and/or sprouting them first.

Spotlight on Sweet Cassava

Sweet Cassava is a long root vegetable that has white flesh and a dark, rough outer skin. This nutty-flavoured, starchy vegetable is high in fibre, carbohydrates and nutrients and is commonly used in South American and West Indian cooking. It is grown in tropical regions of the world, can withstand difficult growing conditions and may also be known as yuca or manioc.

The most commonly consumed part of the vegetable is the root, which is very versatile, benefits from being gluten-free, grain-free and nut-free and is used to make cassava flour and tapioca starch, which is ideal for thickening sauces. It is important to note that cassava in its raw form contains cyanogenic glycosides, which can turn into cyanide in the body, so should only be consumed cooked. Due to detoxification processes, commercially available cassava flours and tapioca starches do not have any harmful levels of cyanide but should be cooked before consumption.

Sweet Cassava can be prepared in a similar way to a potato. It can be bought prepared and frozen, but if bought fresh, look for a firm texture and a dry outer skin.

To prepare:

1. Scrub the root and wash thoroughly
2. Peel and cut into chunks, removing the fibrous inner core
3. Soak in a bowl of water to reduce cyanide content and prevent discolouration
4. Wash thoroughly and cook well—boil, steam, roast or fry until tender

10 Ways To Use Sweet Cassava

1. Chips
2. Boiled and served with a dressing
3. Roti
4. Pizza base
5. Crispy coating for chicken, fish, squid or prawns
6. Gnocchi or dumplings
7. Crisps
8. Nachos
9. Crumble
10. Cookies / Biscuits

Sue's Love of Flavour

My love of flavour came from the wonderful creations my parents cooked in our kitchen at home. I grew up, in the UK, with parents that were from the wonderful island of Trinidad. My parents grew up on food that was home grown and prepared fresh every day, cooked on a homemade clay stove, housing a wood fire, which my parents say added to the flavour of the food. They both lived in remote and poor villages, so food was cherished and nothing was wasted. The food we ate growing up was home cooked and full of West Indian flavour, spice and heat. Our food was always prepared with love and as a young child I understood that some of the food I ate at home was very different from what most of my friends at school ate. Food to our family and friends provided connection, love and belonging. Growing up on such flavoursome food and visiting our extended family in Trinidad and Tobago, at a young age my sister and I were lucky enough to have eclectic palates.

One of my favourite childhood foods was crab. I remember at around the age of seven being practised in the art of cracking the claws, picking out every last shred of the beautiful, sweet meat and enjoying each mouthful. We were lucky enough to be able to visit and stay with our relatives in Trinidad and Tobago every few years and my memories of those holidays conjure up the incredible smells and tastes, sights and sounds of the Caribbean. We picked and ate fresh mangoes, drank coconut water and sugar cane juice and even had the opportunity to pick cacao pods, (I remember being quite confused at the time as there was no chocolate inside). All of our gatherings and celebrations as children were centered around food and they still are today.

One of my memories from very early childhood was in Trinidad, meeting some of my aunts and uncles for the first time. My parents came from large families and we had what seemed like a whole day of visiting different relatives who wanted to meet my sister and I. Each relative we visited had taken such care to prepare different dishes, chutneys and pickles for us to enjoy, but I distinctly remember saying to my Mum and Dad halfway through the day that I couldn't visit anyone else as I wasn't able to fit any more food in my tummy!

In the mid 1980's I have early memories of travelling by bus with my mum and sister to different parts of East London to source ingredients such as okra, callaloo, mango, plantain, scotch bonnet chilli peppers, lentils and curry powder from Indian grocery stores for our meals. We didn't eat out very often, but Mum had a great gift of being able to eat food at a restaurant and recreate the flavours at home. This meant that our food at home expanded to Chinese and Thai cuisine by the time we were in our early teens. We used to help Mum and Dad in the kitchen sometimes, but mostly watch them in full flow and devour the end results. There were no notes passed down the generations. Nothing was measured. Everything was done by instinct, smell, taste and touch and that's exactly how I learnt to cook.

I have always loved food, (both cooking and eating!) and I'm lucky that my husband and my children also share this passion. We have always cooked Indian, British, Chinese and Thai food, as well as the Trinidadian food I grew up on. As a family the kitchen really is the most important room in our home, housing numerous spice blends, marinades, noodles, flours, sauces and chillis. Some of these weren't suitable for the elimination phase of my AIP journey, but I found that I used the AIP elimination phase friendly spice ingredients with such care and was amazed by how just using the following few ingredients could create such wonderful flavours:

- Ginger – fresh and powder
- Turmeric – fresh and powder
- Cinnamon – whole sticks and powder
- Clove powder
- Mace powder
- Amchur, amchoor or aamchur powder (green mango powder providing a citrus or tarte flavour)
- Preserved lemons (perfect for adding a distinct flavour but check for added ingredients)
- Onion – fresh and powder
- Garlic – fresh and powder
- Curry leaves – fresh, dried and powder
- Fenugreek leaves – fresh and dried
- Kaffir lime leaves – frozen and dried
- Tamarind – pulp and powder
- Fish sauce – usually made from anchovies, but check for added ingredients
- Anchovies – provides a salty depth to dishes and if blended, can be used as an alternative to fish sauce
- Nutritional yeast – provides a cheesy, nutty flavour with added B vitamins and can be added to soups, roasted with vegetables or used to make cheese sauce or pesto

Spotlight on AIP Flours and Starches

We have already talked about arrowroot powder as a key thickening agent but let's explore a few other flours and starches.

Cassava flour

Cassava flour is derived from the sweet cassava plant and is formed by peeling the outer bark-like skin, grating or grinding and dehydrating. It is high in fibre and carbohydrates, much like a potato and is a great gluten-free alternative. When cassava flour is used in cooking, it has a very similar appearance and texture to wheat flour and forms a neutral base used to create either savoury or sweet dishes.

Tapioca starch

A common assumption is that cassava flour is the same as tapioca flour/starch, however they have distinct differences. Cassava is the whole root whereas tapioca is a starch extracted from the cassava root. It goes through a process of washing and pulping to create a liquid starch, which is then left to evaporate. The remaining flour-like substance is known as tapioca flour, which is ideal for thickening sauces, much like cornflour or arrowroot.

Tiger nut flour

Tiger nut flour is made from milled tiger nuts, which are not nuts at all but small root vegetables. The flour is high in fibre, has a fine texture and is ideal to bake with due to its naturally sweet taste.

Coconut flour

Coconut flour is made from the coconut solids that are left over after the coconut 'meat' has been used to produce coconut milk and is low in carbohydrates and high in fibre. The coconut solids are dried at a low temperature and ground into a fine, flour-like powder, which is suitable for baking cookies and biscuits.

CHAPTER 10

Sharing Food

When deciding to embark on any new eating plan, one of the first fears we encounter is "is this going to isolate me?" and "will I ever be able to enjoy a meal out with friends ever again?"

You might also have a family who are unwilling to make changes to their food and the prospect of having to prepare two completely different meals every day could be enough to stop you from trying.

Let me put your mind at rest, it does NOT have to be this way. Set the intention at the beginning that this is not going to be a difficult process and it's completely normal to want to eat nutritious and healing foods. Rest assured, this is not the end of your social life.

Let's explore how to navigate eating with others during the most challenging part of the process—the initial elimination phase. After this phase, once you have reintroduced more foods back in, there will only be a small number of trigger foods you will want to avoid because of the way they make you feel. The maintenance phase can be much easier to navigate when eating with others.

Let's start with at home, family dining:

Make the majority of the meal the same for everyone

When you look at the recipes in this book and the meals you already prepare for your family you will start to see that most of your shared meals will be palatable for the whole family. Roast chicken with AIP gravy and all the veggies is a staple favourite in our home which we enjoy every week. Casseroles and soups are so easy to make AIP-compliant without anyone noticing.

Another way you approach this is to make a base dish suitable for you, set a portion or two aside for you and then add extra ingredients, such as spices and tomatoes at the end to satisfy the family.

Cook only alternative accompaniments

In the case above, of a shared roast chicken dinner, everyone can share the meat, veggies and gravy. All you need to do is cook roast potatoes for everyone else and roast sweet potatoes for you. No extra time and everyone's plate looks more or less the same. It will stop you feeling like the odd one out or falling into a "poor me, I'm missing out" mindset—more on that in the next chapter.

It's relatively straightforward to make one main AIP dish for the whole family, prepare rice, pasta, bread, noodles or potatoes for everyone else and an alternative vegetable for you.

Use leftovers for you when making off-limits dinners for the family

When the rest of the family are craving something which is completely off limits because it contains so many foods you are avoiding—such as spaghetti bolognaise, rather than make two versions, or prepare two entirely separate meals, I find it much easier to eat leftovers.

Whether you have a lovely Moroccan lamb casserole in the freezer or yesterday's coleslaw and chicken breast in the fridge, pick something easy to reheat for yourself and use meal prep time to focus on one meal—the family meal.

Everyone eats what you eat!

After a few weeks, once you have gained confidence in your ability to produce delicious AIP-compliant meals you may decide to transition the whole family to this way of eating most of the time, especially if inflammation and other autoimmune diseases are present, or you want to reduce the risk of loved ones developing them. Everyone can benefit from eating this way.

This approach is great if your family are quite adventurous eaters and if the burden of meal production falls mostly on your shoulders.

It's not as radical as it sounds and many of my clients end up doing exactly this. Oftentimes, your plate is so much more colourful, flavoursome and appealing to the eye than what the rest of the family is eating, they want to try some of your meal.

Focus on Key Shared Meals

Very often breakfast is a distinctly personal meal which each person makes for themselves and we all have our preferences; lunch is very often eaten away from home—at work or school; leaving just the evening meal that we sit down to share together.

When you consider it this way—that only one third of your meals have to appeal to the family it can switch your mindset from " this is going to be hard" to "I can do this".

Allow the family to enjoy whatever they want for breakfast and lunch, as you focus on your own needs for these meals and come together using the tips above to get creative around dinner time.

Get the family involved if you can

This is especially useful if your children are older and can have several advantages. Firstly, by challenging them to come up with an AIP-compliant meal for the whole family and cook it once a week, you get an evening off!

Secondly, they will come up with new ideas that you wouldn't have thought of and so increase the variety of meals in the family diet. They will think outside the box and even enjoy the challenge, and who knows, it might even introduce them to cooking for the very first time.

Finally, you're teaching your children about preparing a balanced plate, eating nutrient dense and anti-inflammatory foods and showing them that they have the ability to positively impact their health through the food choices they make. Get them reading this book, researching online and empowering themselves through knowledge and healthy habits now, to set them up for a healthy future.

If however, your family resists and doesn't want to get involved then let it go. Don't force them and refocus on this being YOUR healing journey. I can guarantee when they see the change in you, they will be curious about how you did it, even if they don't voice it. You are being an incredible role model by valuing yourself and your health enough to make positive changes. Keep going!

What about eating with friends and eating out?

Meeting for coffee

The best part of meeting up for coffee or lunch is the CONNECTION rather than the food and drink itself, however delicious the menu is. Keep this in mind. It's alright that for a few weeks of your life you might need to choose tea without milk, rooibos or herbal tea instead of the dairy-fest latte and forgo the pastry altogether.

It's a good idea to keep some herbal or fruit tea bags in your handbag. Not all cafes stock them—just ask for hot water. Not all your friends will have them in their pantry either, so save them the embarrassment of discovering a vintage, dusty chamomile teabag and offering you that.

Try to meet up only with the friends who are supportive of your health project during the elimination phase. Those seemingly well-meaning friends who like to say, "come on, one coffee won't hurt you!" are going to undermine your efforts. Save socialising with those people until after you have reintroduced some foods so you can avoid unhelpful conversations. You do not have to justify or defend yourself to anyone and remember—it's not forever!

Change the Lunch Venue

If you have regular catch ups with friends at restaurants where you know the food isn't going to work for you, suggest something new. Why not meet up for a walk instead and bring a picnic. You still get the social connection, still eat on plan and you have the additional benefits of some gentle exercise and fresh air as well.

If your illness doesn't allow for even the gentlest of walks yet, see if you can find a picnic spot in your area where you can park close by and still benefit from fresh air.

Other ideas might be to meet to have a craft afternoon together, go to the cinema (bring your own snacks) or my favourite—invite them over to your house, where you can be in control of the food.

Entertain at Home

The easiest way to keep to the diet and still socialise is to have your friends over to you. You control the food ingredients and you can cook something non-AIP for them. Even better, cook a completely AIP-compliant meal for everyone.

One of my most inspiring clients, Debbie, was an absolute star at this. Debbie came to me with Rheumatoid Arthritis and had been surviving (barely) with daily prescription painkillers for four years but they were not completely helping the pain.

Debbie is a mother of two gorgeous young women and a young, glamorous grandmother to two grandchildren. Along with her husband, she runs their growing business. Despite the pain she was experiencing, Debbie loves to socialise, particularly cooking for friends and family almost every weekend. When COVID restrictions hit in 2020, like many people, her stress levels went through the roof as they tried to keep everything going, especially the business and of course her symptoms worsened.

On Day 10 of her elimination phase she messaged me in a state of glee to say that for the first time in four years she did not have to start her day with those prescription painkillers. She couldn't believe it at first and thought it was a one-off event and that tomorrow she would be back on the pills again. Her fears were unfounded—she didn't have to take those drugs again, until just recently after catching COVID which caused her condition to briefly flare.

Once she started feeling great, that was it! She was 100% committed to the diet. Having so many demands on her time, Debbie had already embraced batch cooking, making all the lunches on a Sunday for her and her husband for the work week ahead, so she took to that really easily.

What I really love about Debbie's story was she was uncompromising about how she was nourishing herself. It was her top priority. As the keen cook in the family, she wasn't going to prepare anything other than AIP-compliant meals.

After the lockdown ended, she returned to having friends and family over for dinner but all the food was AIP-compliant. The only exception was that they drank wine and she abstained. Her guests would taste the delicious food, she would tell them it was all part of her AIP program and they couldn't believe it. None of her guests missed wheat or dairy or any of the other ingredients we have just become habituated to eating. They got spoiled with Debbie's delicious and healthy food.

Eating at Restaurants

Eating out can be problematic because there are so many foods which are off limits in the early weeks. In time, you will be able to have some foods, quite happily from time to time (and enjoy them all the more when you do—proper treats!) Many restaurants these days are used to accommodating different dietary needs, although they might baulk at the AIP list of foods to avoid if you show them that!

You can call the restaurant ahead of time to ask if they can accommodate wheat and dairy free and most of them are more than happy to do this. I have had some very generous chefs help me out over the years. I think they actually get bored cooking the same menu all the time and enjoy the new challenge.

Pick clean and simple foods, such as steak or fish and salad with dressing on the side (bring your own dressing with you!) Even seemingly simple foods can have hidden ingredients, flavourings, thickeners and inflammatory cooking oils so you may still get a reaction even to what appear to be "clean" foods.

Don't stress. I cannot emphasise this enough. Worrying about it will do more harm to your digestion and immune system than inadvertently consuming some sunflower oil. Do the best you can, enjoy your food and most importantly, enjoy the company.

I do a full elimination month about once a year and I find it's easier to avoid eating out during this time but armed with the tips above, you can navigate every scenario with grace and ease. And remember, this is only for a few weeks of your life and things will get easier after that.

Eating at a Friend's House

This has the potential to be the trickiest one to navigate. On the one hand it's your friend and they will understand that you are eating to improve your health and be right behind you one hundred percent.

On the other hand, you might be invited to eat at someone's house you don't know well or have a tricky relationship with.

Then there is the feeling that you don't want to stress out the host by giving them a list of dietary requirements as long as your arm. Put their minds at ease first of all by letting them know that you can eat many things—meat, fish, vegetables and salads are all fine.

I always offer to bring a dish to contribute to the meal (AIP of course) to take the pressure off the host. A salad is always welcome and you can literally gorge yourself on it, in the unlikely situation that you cannot eat anything they have prepared.

Since desserts are tricky due to their over-reliance on added sugar and dairy, it's a good idea to bring a dessert to share, which everyone—but most importantly, you—can enjoy. See some of the sweet treat options in Part 3.

I am lucky in that I have never been a great fan of dessert, with the exception of custard—check out the recipe for this in Part 3, it's delicious! So, over the past 50+ years, I have become very comfortable and familiar with politely declining pudding. If you have filled up on your main course, this is completely socially acceptable to do, so don't fear offending if you decline dessert. Simply complement the host on how delicious it looks but you are just too full.

Navigating special dinners and celebrations

Holidays, vacations, birthdays and weddings can throw us curve balls. However, there will always be these events on the horizon so please don't use one impending event to stop you from getting started now. Keep these events in perspective, relative to your bigger health goal which is to start feeling better—to have more energy, less pain, clear skin and a clear head, not to mention returning to your body's optimum weight.

If you eat 3 meals a day, that's 1095 meals in a year. So, for meals like Christmas and birthdays—remember it's just one meal and you can always go all out next year. A two-week vacation might be more challenging to work with, in which case you might prefer to start your elimination after you return. But, with that said you can still find a way to do both, especially if you are self-catering.

Another of my most successful clients, Rachel, began her elimination phase on December 23rd, two days before Christmas and she has three children. She stuck to it and ate lots of roast dinners over the holidays, which the whole family was delighted about. She had the extra bonus of not needing to unpick all the "damage" of feasting on excessive cheese and chocolate over the holiday period.

Don't let future commitments stop you from beginning now, in three months' time you'll be so glad you started when you did.

CHAPTER 11

Nourishment Not Punishment

Have you ever "gone on a diet" before? Chances are high that you have.

Have you ever been told there was something wrong with your appearance and that you didn't look "right"? Again, unless you have been very lucky, chances are that you have.

We are bombarded with stereotypes around how we should look, how we should feel and how we should behave. It begins in childhood and continues day in, day out. In today's era of social media there is more pressure than ever before to appear looking "perfect" and to be living the "perfect" life.

All these expectations can become internalised and if you look deeply enough you might find them showing up in your own self-talk as "I am not good enough as I am" and "there is something wrong with me".

It's nonsense of course and your conscious mind knows this and can rationalise it as nonsense. The trouble is the conscious mind only controls 5% of your life, the rest is controlled by your subconscious. 95% of everything you do is controlled just below the level of your awareness and runs your life through your automatic and largely unseen habits of behaviour and your habits of thinking.

If you really want to heal and make changes that will stick, you need to look at your habitual behaviour but especially your habitual thoughts. Your internal dialogue tells you about your self-identity and only habits which align with your sense of identity will become permanent. So, if you want to have new, positive habits which run automatically without any need for willpower, it's time to look at how you see and define yourself. Change this and everything else becomes easy to change.

Let's look at some past behaviour for some insight.

If you have embarked on a diet or eating plan before, ask yourself the following questions. Take some time over this and journal your answers. (If you haven't ever been on a diet, think about another situation where you were trying to make positive changes).

- What was the motivation behind the diet?
- Was it to lose weight or to get healthy?
- What was your attitude during the diet?
- Was it a punishment or an act of self-love?
- Was it a short-term fix that once achieved, would allow you to go back to old habits?
- Was it approached with force or patience?
- Did you at any point feel like a victim, that life was unfair?
- Did you fight the process?
- Did the diet work? Did the results stick?
- Did you sabotage your own efforts by overindulging in something you were trying to avoid?

If you answered yes to the last question, how did that make you feel?

Your relationship with food is very complex. It's a reflection of the relationship you have with yourself, with others and with your life.

At the Institute of Integrative Nutrition, where I studied, they follow the principle that there are two forms of food—primary food and secondary food. The food you have on your plate is secondary food, so it's nourishment that upholds the body and all that it needs to do each day. However, primary food, considered more important, covers all the ways you are nourished (or not) by your life.

A healthy life is often described as "a healthy diet and lifestyle"—the "diet" is the nourishment from the food on your plate and the "lifestyle" is everything else that nourishes your life.

Primary food includes such things as the quality of your closest relationships, social life, how fulfilling your career is, how much you exercise, learn new things, engage in creative pursuits and spiritual practices.

Poor nourishment in secondary food which shows up on your plate as poor food choices, almost always has its origin in a lack of nourishment in one or more areas of primary food. We try to compensate for this lack of primary nourishment with behaviours such as comfort eating, disordered eating and cravings.

Consider the following list and rate each area of your life at this point in time, in terms of happiness or fulfilment, with 1 being low and 10 being it couldn't be better, it's great!

________	Primary Relationship
________	Other Important Relationships (such as with your children)
________	Social Life
________	Career Fulfilment
________	Learning New Things
________	Creative Pursuits
________	Spiritual Practices and Connection to Something Bigger
________	Financial Fulfilment
________	Home Environment
________	Home Cooking
________	Exercise/Movement
________	Time Spent Outdoors/Being in Nature
________	Health
________	Joy/Fun

As you review this list, what stands out? Are there any areas which score really high? Great! Keep doing those things. Are there any which score really low?

Chances are, there are some low scoring areas. As you focus on these, notice what kind of thoughts flow through your mind. It can be a really good idea to write these down, free-writing without censorship, judgement or editing. As you read it back you get to see a glimpse of parts of your self-identity. Maybe you wrote things like "I haven't got time or money for that" or "I have no choice but to do the job I do" or "I hate exercise". Each of your statements create a limitation, beyond which you cannot pass. Any time you try to introduce a habit to fix a problem that doesn't align with your sense of identity you struggle. As soon as you run out of willpower, or you reach your goal, the new habit will stop and you will drop back into your old habits which do align with your identity.

Reaching your goal is an interesting one. So many people embark on a weight loss diet, reach their target weight and within months are back to where they started. When you are striving for something it can motivate you to adopt healthy habits but on the day you get on the scales and see your goal has been met—what will motivate you to keep up the good habits? Nothing. Without changing your self-identity from "I struggle with my weight" to "I easily maintain my ideal weight through my food choices" the original habits kick straight back in—habits which align with "I struggle with my weight". And so the years of yo-yo dieting begins.

Go back again and look at your scores for primary food. This time before you jump to criticise yourself or jump into your story about why they score low, I want you to simply take a moment to own it. Free from judgement, justification or resistance, simply recognise that at this point in your life there are some areas in your life which are not nourishing you, they may even be toxic.

Being able to take ownership of all of your life without judgement and take an inventory of where you are right now, is the first step to making the necessary changes to get you back on track. That kind of honesty takes courage and isn't as easy as it sounds. Once you acknowledge where you are, there is a lot you can do to create more primary nourishment in your life. It may require some difficult decisions, changes and choices, such as unpicking the limiting beliefs you hold about yourself, your life and your options. When you change your story as well as cultivate new habits of behaviour which align with your new story, you ABSOLUTELY CAN make changes that stick.

Create behaviours which align with the new version of you, show up as that person in the world through those new behaviours and the end result will take care of itself. This is a big, but essential undertaking and is beyond the scope of this book.

For now, know that addressing only the food on your plate, although it makes a huge impact, will never be enough to counteract all the negative self-talk going on in your head or the constantly triggered stress response you have been ignoring for too long.

As you embark on this new way of eating, change the story around food and remember that the food on your plate is a reflection of all the other areas in your life and your mental diet. What thoughts are you habitually chewing on, over and over again? By changing your food and starting to remove or reduce many of the symptoms which come with gut dysfunction and autoimmunity, you can take your power back. In doing so, you can reclaim ALL areas of your life and even rekindle a long-forgotten sense of purpose again. This is the deepest and most authentic healing you can have.

Working in this integrated way is a fast track to wellbeing—body, mind and spirit and may require some expert help along the way as you explore all these areas of primary nourishment. It's not a weakness to ask for help, it's courageous.

When I designed my three-month program for bringing healing back to people with autoimmune disease, I knew that to bring you back to wholeness you would need to incorporate the AIP diet, stress resilience techniques and deep enquiry into your limiting beliefs and self-sabotaging habits to ensure you don't slip back into old ways ever again.

As the topic of this book, however, is about food, let us return there. Begin by reframing the ideas and beliefs you may have around the word "diet".

In the dictionary, "diet" is described as:

1. something provided or experienced repeatedly
2. the kinds of food that a person, animal, or community habitually eats

Both these definitions describe a diet as a "habit". It's what we habitually eat day in, day out and is influenced by cues, culture, location and upbringing. We also have a diet of thoughts and other behaviours we experience repeatedly, so it's not a word that is restricted to food. It's anything you repeatedly let in—through all of your senses and from within your own mind. It's what you watch on TV, read, whose ideas you allow to influence you, whose beliefs you have accepted as your own and so on.

Somewhere along the way, the word diet changed from "habitual eating" to "a temporary, restrictive weight loss fix"—the complete opposite of a habit because as soon as the "problem" is "fixed" the habitual eating patterns flood back in and more often than not, the person ends up back where they started.

Why? Because your self-identity is not changing and so you're stuck in a repetitive loop of symptoms, punishment and quick fixes.

So, as you contemplate the beginning of the AIP program, ask yourself the following questions again:

- What is the motivation behind this diet, at this point in time?
- Is it to lose weight or to get healthy?
- What is your attitude behind changing the food you eat?
- Is this an act of self-love?
- Do you see yourself going back to old habits once this diet is "over"?
- Are you approaching this with force or patience?
- Do you feel like a victim or do you feel you are taking back some control?
- Do you feel you will slip back to old ways?
- Who do you want to become?
- How does that person live their life? What daily habits does that person have?

Some Mindset Tricks to Help You Succeed

Keeping a supportive mindset during the transition to a new, vitality-building way of eating is half of the battle. Below, I share some of the mindset practices and habits which I have personally found useful and which I share with my clients.

Focus on what you are adding in

If you focus all your attention on what you can't have you will strengthen feelings of punishment, poor me and a sense of identity that says, "I am a victim". Victims by definition do not succeed, so focus your attention on what you are adding into your diet rather than the foods that are being excluded. Focus on building meals that fit with the AIP Plate. This has two benefits: firstly, by flooding your plate with nutrient-rich foods you are having a dramatic, positive impact on your nutritional status, which means a move towards greater health. You will start to feel better sooner because the body has all it needs to run efficiently. As you start to feel better it will build your belief in yourself and your capacity to positively influence the way you feel—no more victim! This strengthens your new self-identity.

And secondly, by filling your plate with all the good stuff there's naturally no room left for the bad stuff. Those foods which you are excluding are simply crowded out without needing to become excessively focussed on avoiding them. It is amazing how this mental trick of crowding out and focusing on the additional foods can make the AIP transition so much easier.

Remember the initial detox symptoms are temporary

Most people feel worse for a few days before they start to feel better. You have not failed if you experience a temporary worsening of symptoms. This is actually a positive thing—signs that your body is letting go of addictive food which have been holding you hostage for years.

Try to celebrate this phase and remind yourself that you have entered a positive process and these symptoms will soon pass.

Don't let the diet create stress

When I have talked to people who have tried the AIP diet (or any diet for that matter) and then given up, one of the common things I hear is that trying to figure out what to eat, how to cook and how to afford it on a budget created too much stress and made the whole endeavour unproductive.

Yes, this can easily happen if you let it. So, be prepared for this potential obstacle and get it out of the way now. Change the story from "this is stressful" to "I easily nourish myself every day" and repeat it to yourself often throughout the day. Remember? No more victim!

This way of eating may be new to you, but it's the diet of your ancestors. If you have been relying on processed and convenience foods for a long time, it can take a little time to get into a rhythm with this, but remind yourself that you can do it.

STEP 1: from the list of nutrient dense foods to include there will be many foods you already eat—so start by simply eating more of these and eating them more often.

STEP 2: step 1 is going to get boring fast! But sadly, many people get stuck here. So, the next step is to review the nutrient dense food list and start including foods you like but don't eat very often. You can literally double the variety in your diet with this step.

STEP 3: pick one or two new foods from the nutrient dense food list to try each week. Some of these new foods may well become new staples as you discover new flavours and textures. If you try something and don't like it, never mind, move on. You are not expected to like everything.

When it comes to budget follow this approach: pick the best quality your budget will allow:

If the best is out of reach, select "better" options. An example might be:

BEST: Organic grass fed/pasture raised/wild meat (any variety)

BETTER: Lean cuts of conventionally raised (grain fed) meat and farmed fish

GOOD: Any meat or fish without artificial additives and flavourings

And then let yourself be ok with that.

When people say "I can't do AIP because it's too expensive" I challenge them to check out liver the next time they are at the supermarket. Liver is one of the most nutrient dense foods on the planet, it's so good for you and it's one of the cheapest cuts of meat you can buy. That's a double win. You'll see several liver recipes in Part 3, because it is such an important part of a nutrient dense, anti-inflammatory diet.

Tinned tuna, mackerel and sardines are another example of a good choice—they are all nutrient dense, anti-inflammatory and inexpensive. They have the additional benefit that they will store for months. Having a few tins of tuna in your pantry means you can always reach for something in a hunger emergency that will not sabotage your new eating plan. The other debate is around whether or not to buy organic fruits and vegetables. Again, I would use the same approach. If it's in your budget, then organic is best but even highly sprayed vegetables are going to be better than eating no vegetables at all so long as you wash them.

A "better" or compromise position to take might be to review the CLEAN FIFTEEN and the DIRTY DOZEN lists. The Dirty Dozen is a list of fruits and vegetables which are the most highly sprayed with chemicals. Try to buy these organic if you can, especially when they are in season and generally more affordable.

The Clean Fifteen are the most minimally sprayed so buying these as conventionally grown produce is pretty safe—don't waste your money buying organic for these unless your budget stretches to it.

These two lists vary from year to year and from country to country, so search on the internet to find the current one for your region.

As your energy returns, consider turning over some of your garden or even a windowsill to grow your own food. You can have a wonderful selection of herbs on a kitchen windowsill, fresh lettuce in a flower tub outside your door with little space or time required.

I am always hungry!

Get ahead of the game when it comes to hunger and cravings so you don't allow these feelings to sabotage you. With chronic illness it is not uncommon for your hunger and satiety hormones to be out of balance. In my experience these regulate quite quickly when eating the AIP way. If you are often feeling hungry, it is likely that you are either not eating enough or you need to review the AIP plate.

When I hear this from clients, we review their food diary and it usually comes down to just a handful of things:

- Not eating enough and your body is crying out for fuel and nutrients
- Grazing throughout the day rather than having defined eating and non-eating times. Grazing can disrupt hunger hormones and drive inflammation
- Not eating enough healthy fat and animal protein in a meal. These two components take longer to digest than carbohydrate from fruits and vegetables. By including them in every meal you slow down the transit time of food, leaving you feeling full for longer
- Out of date beliefs about animal meat and fats being "bad" making it challenging for you to incorporate them into your meals and relying only on vegetables
- Cravings for something sweet, especially in the afternoon. These cravings will subside by including more animal protein earlier in the day
- The feelings of hunger can actually be feelings of thirst, so be sure to drink more water. As you eat more fibre than you are used to you will also need to increase your water intake to avoid constipation.

Reframe food as an act of self-love

The diet/punishment paradigm is so deeply embedded in our culture that it can be hard to overcome. I remember when I was addressing my Hashimoto's Thyroiditis with AIP and had some routine blood tests taken to track the progress, the results showed dramatic improvement and I was thrilled. I shared the results with some friends, telling them just how successful my diet and stress management approach had been, and their response took me by surprise. There was almost a sense that I was some sort of strange superhero. They responded with comments like:

> "You are so brave, not many people would take such a radical approach to getting well."
>
> "I couldn't have changed my diet like that, I like bread too much."
>
> "Why not just take medication?"

Funny isn't it, that we collectively see nourishing ourselves well as being "radical". Well, I guess I'm a radical then because I love cabbage and feeling great more than I like a cheese sandwich made with white bread. [True fact—before I adopted the AIP way, a cheese toasted sandwich on white bread, with chips was my favourite thing to order when having lunch out—I know, sophisticated, eh? Now I look at a cheese sandwich and don't even register it as food.]

Do you have a pet? If you do, how do you choose their food? Even if it's purely based on cost, take a look at the packaging and read the blurb. There will be big bold statements about how it contains everything your pet needs to thrive—all the nutrition for vitality and a healthy coat. When it comes to our pets, we intrinsically know that we owe it to them (as their only nourishment providers) to give them what their bodies need.

Why don't we do that for ourselves?

Another way to look at it might be to imagine that your child, or any loved one, was told they needed to eat in a particular way in order to get well and to recover from an illness. Wouldn't you go all out to make sure they were being fed exactly what they needed?

If you are reading this book, then the chances are high that you are unwell. Feed yourself as you would feed your poorly child, close family member or your pet. And if you struggle with that, examine which part of your self-identity is saying you don't deserve that kind of loving treatment and strive to heal that wounded part of yourself.

Nourish yourself as an act of self-love and you'll be able to nourish and love others from your overflowing cup.
We have now gone through all the theory, made some preparations and thought about the attitude we are bringing to this next step. Now it's time for the best bit—getting into action, cooking and enjoying delicious and nutritious dishes!

All the information in this book and all the information in the world is utterly worthless until it is IMPLEMENTED.

In Part 3, you will find plenty of mouth-watering delights, some of which will become household staples to enjoy every week and others saved for more special occasions or when sharing AIP food with friends and family.

All these recipes have been perfected in our very own kitchens and eaten regularly in our homes. We hope you enjoy them, adapt them, improve them and share them with your loved ones.

If at any time during your elimination phase you hit an obstacle or you feel stuck and uninspired we hope you return to this book as a guide and a trusted resource. Turn to it for new food ideas and review Part 2 to see which obstacle you have encountered and how to quickly move past it.

We wish you improved health and happiness and hope you enjoy nourishing yourself in a whole new way and with a whole new mindset.

Good luck!

PART 3

DELICIOUS AIP RECIPES

OFFAL

BONE BROTH

EASY

PREP: 15 MINUTES
COOKING: 12 to 24 HOURS

1 ½ LITRES

SLOW COOKER OR
LARGE STOCK POT

This broth is packed with nutrients and can be made from any leftover bones to make a nourishing hot beverage to sip from a mug, or added to soups, gravies and stews.

Hint: It will keep in the fridge for a week and can also be frozen in small portions.

INGREDIENTS

1 chicken carcass or other bones

1 brown onion – skin on and quartered

2 carrots – unpeeled and chopped into large chunks

2 stalks of celery chopped into large chunks

3 garlic cloves – skin on

3 sprigs of fresh rosemary or a heaped tsp of dried

3 sprigs fresh thyme or a heaped tsp of dried

2 fresh or dried bay leaves

2 TBSP cloudy apple cider vinegar

1 ½ to 2 litres water

1 tsp turmeric powder

COOKING STEPS

1. Place the chicken carcass or other bones into a slow cooker or a large stock pot on the stove.
2. Add all of the ingredients to the bones except for the turmeric and completely cover with a generous amount of water.
3. If cooking on the stove top cover with a lid and bring to the boil, then reduce heat to a gentle simmer for 12–24 hours. You may need to top up the water part way through.
4. If using a slow cooker cover with a lid and leave to simmer for 12–24 hours.
5. During the last hour of simmering add 1 teaspoon of turmeric powder.

OLWEN'S CHICKEN LIVERS IN GARLIC & COCONUT MILK

EASY
PREP: 10 MINUTES
COOKING: 25 MINUTES
SERVES 2
FRYING PAN OR WOK

This is a lovely way to eat liver. As another option you may like to throw in some fresh sage, thyme, or oregano to replace the coriander. This will add variety to the taste and the nutrient intake.

INGREDIENTS

2 TBSP duck fat (or goose fat)

1 large onion diced

3–4 cloves garlic thickly sliced

450g chicken liver

5 or 6 mushrooms roughly chopped

4 rashers bacon roughly chopped

1 large bunch fresh coriander chopped

½ cup coconut milk

½ cup bone broth heated

Salt to taste

COOKING STEPS

1. In a large frying pan, heat 1 TBSP of the duck fat and sweat off the onions before adding the garlic to cook gently for a few minutes. Remove from the heat and decant into a bowl.
2. Add the remainder of the duck fat to the pan with the liver and fry on a medium heat for 5 to 10 minutes. Whilst the liver is cooking add the mushrooms and bacon to brown a little.
3. Return the onion and garlic to the pan and mix all together. Allow to fry until the liver is cooked to taste, turning it occasionally (up to 20 minutes in total).
4. Near the end, add the coriander, coconut milk and heated bone broth and warm through. Season with salt to taste.

CHICKEN LIVER, HERB & MUSHROOM PÂTÉ

EASY
PREP: 10 MINUTES
COOKING: 15 MINUTES
SERVES 4
FRYING PAN, BLENDER & GRATER

Before my AIP journey I only really ate liver in the form of pâté at Christmas time and had no desire to eat it more frequently than once a year. I now LOVE liver and enjoy eating a batch of this pâté every week. It is perfect for a lunch or a snack on the go with slices of granny smith apple, cucumber, celery or carrot sticks. I always feel so good after eating it as it is filled with amazing nutrients and herbs that will leave you wanting more. —*Sue*

Hint: If you are not used to eating liver try chicken, lamb or calves liver to see which you prefer. This recipe can be cooked with any of these. I recommend adding 8 to 10 drops of food grade essential oils (I like lemon or orange) for a fresh and zingy taste.

Storage hint: Once made the pâté can be stored in portions in the freezer and taken out to defrost as required.

INGREDIENTS

380g chicken liver

3 TBSP olive oil

1 large onion finely sliced

1 TBSP ginger finely chopped

4 cloves garlic finely chopped

2 rashers prosciutto chopped

3 medium chestnut mushrooms finely sliced

1 TBSP fresh sage or ½ TBSP dried

1 TBSP fresh thyme or ½ TBSP dried

1 TBSP fresh rosemary or ½ TBSP dried

½ TBSP fresh oregano or ¼ TBSP dried

¼ tsp pink Himalayan salt

1 TBSP garlic powder

½ TBSP onion powder

½ tsp maple syrup

1 tsp organic apple cider vinegar

8 to 10 drops of food grade essential oils (lemon or orange) or 1 lemon or orange zested

COOKING STEPS

1 Wash the chicken livers and pat dry with kitchen paper. Remove and discard any fat and sinew and cut the liver into evenly sized pieces (approximately 4 to 5 cm) and set aside.

2 Heat 2 TBSP of the oil in large frying pan and fry the onion and ginger on a medium to high heat for 4 to 5 minutes until softened and slightly brown. Lower the heat and add the garlic and prosciutto and fry for approximately 2 to 3 minutes, taking care not to burn the garlic.

3 Next, to the pan add the finely sliced mushrooms and herbs and fry for 5 to 6 minutes until the mushrooms have browned slightly. Add salt to taste, stir well and decant onto a plate to cool.

4 In the same pan add the remaining 1 TBSP of oil and heat on a medium to high heat. Add the liver and season with salt, garlic and onion powder stirring well. Lightly sauté the seasoned liver for 1–2 minutes on each side or until seared and lightly golden.

5 Add in the maple syrup, stir and well and de-glaze the pan with the apple cider vinegar. Once the liver is cooked to your liking, decant into a blender with the cooled and cooked mushrooms and herbs and blend into a smooth paste.

6 Taste and adjust seasoning if required. If adding food grade essential oils add 8 to 10 drops of lemon or orange oil or the zest of one lemon or orange.

7 Stir well and transfer every last mouthful into small storage containers. Serve with apple slices, cucumber, celery or carrot sticks. If storing, cool and refrigerate or freeze.

LIVER, WITH PLANTAIN, MUSHROOMS & SPINACH

EASY
PREP: 10 MINUTES
COOKING: 15 MINUTES
SERVES 2
FRYING PAN OR WOK

If I have days where my energy has dipped, liver is always what I gravitate towards to give me a nutrient boost. Served with pan fried ripe plantain this gives the dish a sweet and savoury flavour that is also a good source of magnesium and potassium.

—Sue

If yellow ripe plantain is not available you can easily substitute with small slices of sweet potato or a slightly unripe banana.

INGREDIENTS

LIVER

380g chicken liver

3 TBSP olive oil

1 large onion finely sliced

1 TBSP ginger finely chopped

4 cloves garlic finely chopped

2 rashers prosciutto chopped

3 medium chestnut mushrooms finely sliced

1 TBSP fresh sage or ½ TBSP dried

1 TBSP fresh thyme or ½ TBSP dried

1 TBSP fresh rosemary or ½ TBSP dried

½ TBSP fresh oregano or ¼ TBSP dried

Salt to taste (pink Himalayan)

1 TBSP garlic powder

½ TBSP onion powder

½ tsp maple syrup

1 tsp organic apple cider vinegar

PLANTAIN

1 TBSP olive oil

1 ripe plantain sliced

¼ tsp pink Himalayan salt

1 tsp garlic powder ½ tsp onion powder

SPINACH

1 large handful baby spinach

COOKING STEPS

1. Wash the chicken livers and pat dry with kitchen paper. Remove and discard any fat and sinew and cut the liver into evenly sized 4 cm pieces and set aside.
2. Heat 2 TBSP of the oil in large frying pan and fry the onion and ginger for 4 to 5 minutes until softened and slightly brown. Turn the heat down to medium and add the garlic and prosciutto and fry for approximately 2 to 3 minutes, taking care not to burn the garlic.
3. Next, to the pan add the finely sliced mushrooms and herbs and fry for 5 to 6 minutes until the mushrooms have browned slightly. Add salt to taste, stir well and decant into a bowl to cool.
4. In the same pan add the remaining TBSP of oil and heat on a medium to high heat. Add the liver and season with salt, garlic and onion powder. Lightly sauté the seasoned liver for 1–2 minutes on each side until seared and lightly golden.
5. Add the maple syrup, stir well and de-glaze the pan with the apple cider vinegar. Once the liver is cooked to your liking, decant into the bowl with the cooked mushrooms and stir.

PLANTAIN

6. Wash and dry the pan, add the oil and heat on a medium to high heat. Add the slices of plantain and season with salt, garlic and onion powder.
7. Cook on each side for 2 to 3 minutes until seared and lightly caramelised and crispy, or to your personal taste. Decant onto a serving plate.

SPINACH

8. Wash and dry the spinach and cook in the same pan on a medium heat until wilted. Serve immediately with the liver and plantain.

LIVER & BACON CASSEROLE

EASY
PREP: 5 MINUTES
COOKING: 40 MINUTES
SERVES 4
LARGE FRYING PAN AND CASSEROLE DISH

This dish is so nutritious and full of flavour. I crave it at least once a week and miss it when I haven't eaten it in a while. It is one of those dishes that makes you feel good, knowing you have fed your body so many vitamins and nutrients in one meal. It is lovely for breakfast the next day warmed up with some shredded spinach, or if there is not much left, add more broth for a nutritious soup. —*Claire*

Hint: Use a stove and oven compatible casserole dish so the dish can be prepared on the stove and then transferred to the oven, but you can easily use a frying pan and transfer the ingredients to a casserole dish for cooking in the oven.

INGREDIENTS

- 2 TBSP olive oil
- 2 large onions sliced
- 500g liver
- 1 carrot sliced
- 4 mushrooms sliced
- 1 cup home-made bone broth
- 1 TBSP coconut aminos
- 4 tsp fresh sage or 2 tsp dried sage
- 1 tsp fresh thyme or ½ tsp dried thyme
- 1 tsp fresh rosemary or ½ tsp dried rosemary
- 1 packet bacon (streaky or back)
- 1 sweet potato very thinly sliced

COOKING STEPS

1. Preheat your oven to 180°C (fan).
2. Heat the olive oil in a large pan and sauté the sliced onions.
3. Add in the whole pieces of liver and sauté for 2 minutes each side to lightly brown.
4. Add in the sliced carrots and mushrooms, cover with homemade bone broth and add the coconut aminos.
5. Stir in the sage, thyme and rosemary and bring to the boil.
6. If using a frying pan, transfer the contents to a casserole dish.
7. In the casserole dish, layer the bacon across the top of the liver and onion mixture.
8. Top with a layer of finely sliced sweet potato.
9. Either cover and cook on the stove until the vegetables are soft (up to 30 minutes), or pop in the oven at 180°C for up to 30 minutes depending on the size of your liver pieces—larger pieces will remain soft and not rubbery.

บาท
2524

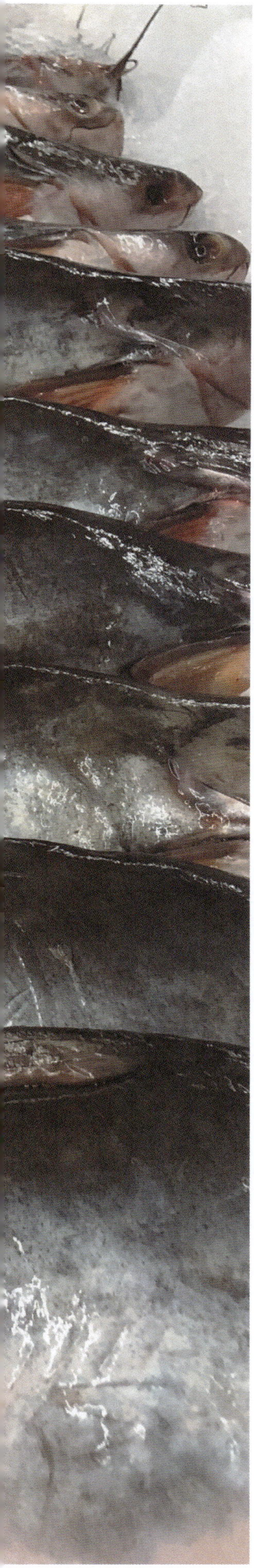

FISH & SEAFOOD

CRISPY GARLIC PRAWNS

EASY

PREP: 15 MINUTES
COOKING: 20 MINUTES

SERVES 4

FRYING PAN OR WOK

This dish was created from a craving for spicy pepper prawns from a local Chinese restaurant. It is a mouth-watering AIP alternative and really hits the spot when you fancy something special that you can share. —*Sue*

INGREDIENTS

750g large raw peeled prawns

4 TBSP cassava flour (you may require slightly more or less depending on your brand of flour)

1 tsp pink Himalayan salt

1 TBSP garlic powder

3 TBSP extra virgin olive oil (may need more oil depending on how many batches you require)

3 large spring onions (red or green)

5 large cloves garlic chopped

1 ½ TBSP fresh ginger coarsely grated

COOKING STEPS

1. Dry the prawns with kitchen paper and set aside. In a large bowl mix the cassava flour, salt and garlic powder and stir in the prawns, coating them thoroughly.
2. Heat the oil in a large non-stick frying pan and add small batches of the coated prawns, taking care not to overload your pan. Fry on a high heat, stirring occasionally until the prawns turn pink and have a crispy golden coating on both sides.
3. Decant the cooked prawns onto kitchen paper to absorb any excess oil. Finely slice the garlic, ginger & spring onions and fry in the same pan on a high heat for 2 to 3 minutes until softened. Mix with the prawns and enjoy whilst hot.

THAI-INSPIRED SALMON POACHED IN COCONUT & LEMONGRASS

EASY
PREP: 20 MINUTES
COOKING: 10 MINUTES
SERVES 2
LARGE FRYING PAN OR WOK

This would be a wonderful addition to any dinner party or whenever you fancy something exotic and special.

INGREDIENTS

1 TBSP coconut oil

½ small red onion sliced

1 can coconut milk (400ml)

1–2 inches fresh ginger roughly sliced

1 lemongrass stalk split lengthwise (if unavailable use 1–2 drops food grade lemongrass essential oil)

2 tsp coconut aminos

5–6 fresh kaffir lime leaves, crumpled or torn to release flavour

Large handful button mushrooms

2 salmon fillets – unskinned and cut into 1 inch cubes

1 TBSP chopped coriander leaves to garnish

1 lime, quartered, to garnish

COOKING STEPS

1. In a large pan or wok heat the coconut oil and gently soften the onion until it's translucent but not brown.
2. Pour in the coconut milk and reduce to a medium heat as you don't want it to boil too vigorously. It's a delicate ingredient so also don't over stir.
3. Throw in the ginger, lemongrass, coconut aminos and kaffir lime leaves and leave for at least 10 minutes for the flavours to deepen. Add button mushrooms and cook right through.
4. When you are ready to eat, add the salmon cubes and cook for 5 minutes. You want the fish to remain soft and not dry out. Decorate with chopped coriander leaves and lime wedges. (As the lemongrass, ginger and kaffir lime leaves have been left whole or in large slices don't forget to remove these before serving).
5. Serve with cauliflower rice or steamed greens. For non AIP family members, serve with basmati rice and fresh sliced chilis.
6. This coconut and lemongrass base also works well with other fish such as cod, hake, halibut, scallops and prawns.

THAI FISH CURRY WITH DUMPLINGS

MEDIUM
PREP: 10 MINUTES
COOKING: 40 MINUTES
SERVES 2 to 3
BLENDER, FRYING PAN OR WOK, GRATER & SAUCEPAN

INGREDIENTS

THAI CURRY

2 TBSP lemongrass blended

4 cloves garlic blended

2 TBSP ginger blended

6 TBSP fresh coriander blended

2 TBSP water if required

3 large mushrooms chopped

2 TBSP coconut oil

3 shallots sliced

1 ½ cups butternut squash cubed

2 TBSP coconut oil (if required)

1 can coconut milk (400ml) plus up to 200ml water

4 fresh kaffir lime leaves torn

2 TBSP coconut aminos

2 TBSP fish sauce

2 courgettes chopped (2 cups)

1 ½ cups broccoli florets

1 handful spinach

4 to 5 small cod fillets, skinned and cut into cubes

1 lime juiced and zested

1 TBSP chopped coriander

2 TBSP tapioca starch mixed with 2 TBSP water

DUMPLINGS

1 large white sweet potato diced (3 ½ cups)

½ tsp salt

½ TBSP garlic powder

½ cup cassava flour plus up to ½ cup extra for dusting

2 to 6 TBSP olive oil depending on how many batches you have

COOKING STEPS

THAI CURRY

1. Using a food processor or blender blitz the lemongrass, garlic, ginger and coriander into a rough paste, (if required add a little water).
2. In a large frying pan or wok heat 2 TBSP coconut oil and gently fry the shallots until softened. Add the butternut squash and mushrooms and simmer for 5 to 7 minutes with the lid on.
3. Once the butternut squash has softened slightly remove the lid. In the same pan if required add up to 2 TBSP coconut oil and fry the paste for 2 to 3 minutes until it becomes fragrant. Add the coconut milk and kaffir lime leaves and stir well on a gentle simmer. At this point the sauce should turn green.
4. If you would like more sauce half fill your empty can of coconut milk with water and add in with the coconut aminos, fish sauce, chopped courgettes, broccoli florets and chopped cod fillets. To thicken the sauce simmer gently with the tapioca starch and water mix for 4 to 5 minutes until cooked. Throw in a handful of spinach and stir gently; this should wilt within a couple of minutes.

DUMPLINGS

5. Peel, dice and boil the white sweet potato for 10 to 15 minutes until cooked. Drain and mash into a smooth consistency. Add salt and garlic powder and combine well. Gradually add the cassava flour until the mixture forms a dough-like ball. Once the mixture is cool enough to handle coat your hands in a little olive oil to prevent to mixture from sticking to them. Using your hands form small oval shapes and press down on each one lightly with the back of a fork to flatten slightly. Place on a plate sprinkled with cassava flour to prevent the dumplings from sticking.
6. Cook your dumplings on medium heat in batches in a little olive oil, pan frying for 2 to 3 minutes on each side. Once they are a light golden colour serve with your curry topped with some chopped coriander and enjoy.

You know dinner was good when you want to eat it for breakfast the next morning.

This Thai curry has a flavoursome creamy sauce, is full of delicious vegetables and is so comforting with the addition of sweet potato dumplings.

Hint: The kaffir lime leaves release flavour when cooking but don't forget to remove these before serving.

Dumpling hint: You may require slightly more or less cassava flour depending on your brand of flour. The dumplings can easily be made in advance, kept refrigerated and cooked as required, pan frying for a few minutes. You will have a few extra to enjoy as this recipe makes around 40 dumplings in total.

GRILLED MACKEREL & HERB DRESSING

EASY
PREP: 2 MINUTES
COOKING: 5 to 10 MINUTES
SERVES 2
GRILL & BLENDER

This is such a quick fish to cook and is perfect served with Asian-inspired flavours.

INGREDIENTS

2 mackerel fillets

1 tsp olive oil for greasing tray

HERB DRESSING

1 spring onion roughly chopped

3 TBSP fresh coriander roughly chopped

3 TBSP fresh mint roughly chopped

1 TBSP fish sauce

1 lime juiced

COOKING STEPS

1. Turn the grill onto a medium setting to preheat. Score the skin of the mackerel fillets diagonally, approximately 2 cm apart.
2. Place the mackerel on a greased baking tray, skin side up for 5 to 10 mins until the flesh is opaque and cooked through.
3. While the mackerel is under the grill, prepare the dressing ingredients and blend with a hand blender or small food processor to make a dressing. Serve with a salad and enjoy.

SEARED SCALLOPS WITH ROCKET, WATERCRESS AND SPINACH

MEDIUM
15 MINUTES
SERVES 2
LARGE NON-STICK FRYING PAN

This dish was created from an evening shopping trip to my local supermarket, when I noticed these beautiful scallops that were on sale and just waiting to be cooked by me. Cooking scallops isn't as intimidating as it first seems and once you have successfully cooked them once, you will never forget. This dish is perfect for sharing with your most special people.

Hint: Ensure scallops are dry before cooking to achieve a beautiful golden searing. A good non-stick frying pan is best when cooking this dish, but if you don't have one ensure you are using enough oil so the scallops don't stick. —*Sue*

INGREDIENTS

2 TBSP olive oil (you may require more oil depending on your pan)

8–10 scallops including roe

Pink Himalayan or sea salt to taste

2 garlic cloves chopped

1 TBSP balsamic vinegar

2 large handfuls of rocket, watercress and spinach leaves

COOKING STEPS

1. If using scallops from the shell ensure the membrane, grey-brown frill and black thread of intestine are all discarded. Dry the scallops and roe thoroughly to absorb any excess liquid, lightly season with salt on one side and set aside.
2. The key to well-seared scallops is ensuring the pan is hot enough to sear them when they hit the pan. Heat 2 TBSP olive oil in a large non-stick frying pan on a medium-high heat.
3. Add the scallops and roe to the frying pan seasoned side down in a single layer without overcrowding the pan (work in batches if needed). Lightly season the other side with salt and allow them to cook for approximately 2 minutes until they are golden brown on one side. Once they are golden brown carefully turn them over and fry for a couple of minutes on the other side until golden brown and seared.
4. You are looking for the flesh near the top and bottom edges of the scallops to look opaque. Depending on the size of your scallops you may need to adjust your cooking time slightly. When they are cooked remove the scallops and roe from the pan and transfer to a plate.
5. Using the remaining olive oil in the pan, fry the garlic on a medium heat for 1 to 2 minutes until lightly golden, adding the balsamic vinegar to deglaze the pan and create a dressing for the salad.
6. Plate the rocket, watercress and spinach leaves and place the scallops and roe on top. Drizzle over the garlic and balsamic dressing and serve straight away.

CRISPY SQUID

EASY
PREP: 10 MINUTES
COOKING: 20 MINUTES
SERVES 2
WHISK & SMALL DEEP SAUCEPAN

This recipe makes the squid so crispy and is just beautiful served with freshly squeezed lemons.

Hint: This dish was prepared using frozen squid which is so handy as you can just defrost how much you require on the day and it is already cleaned and prepared. Just defrost the rings in a bowl of cold water and dry thoroughly before cooking.

INGREDIENTS

300g prepared squid sliced

2 TBSP garlic powder

¼ tsp pink Himalayan salt

3 cups light olive oil for frying (you may require more oil depending on how many batches you require)

1 lemon cut into wedges

BATTER

¾ cup cassava flour (you may require slightly more or less depending on your brand of flour)

¾ cup tapioca starch

1 cup fizzy water

¼ tsp pink Himalayan salt

COOKING STEPS

1. If using fresh whole squid pull out the tentacles from the main body, cutting below the eye and discarding the innards. Discard the beak and trim the tentacles.
2. Remove the membrane from the body and discard. Pull out the shell or 'quill' and remove the innards by scraping the back of a knife across the body.
3. Wash the squid, taking care to wash away any remaining innards and dry with kitchen paper. Leaving the body whole and clean, slice the squid into 1 cm rings and set aside.
4. If using frozen squid rings defrost and pat dry using kitchen paper.
5. Sprinkle the rings with garlic powder and salt and mix well.

BATTER

6. In a large bowl mix the cassava flour, tapioca starch, fizzy water and salt. The mixture should look similar to a thick pancake mix.
7. In a deep saucepan heat the light olive oil to 325 to 350°F. Dip small batches of the squid into the batter, then into the hot oil, taking care not to overload your saucepan. Fry for 3 to 4 minutes until the squid rises to the surface of the oil and has a crispy golden coating.
8. Decant the squid rings onto kitchen paper to absorb any excess oil and enjoy. Enjoy whilst hot with a squeeze of fresh lemon.

FISH & CHIPS

MEDIUM

PREP: 20 MINUTES
COOKING: 50 MINUTES

SERVES 4 to 5

WHISK, DEEP SAUCEPAN & OVEN

How could we not put fish and chips in this book?

It is such a classic British dish and this batter coats the fish perfectly, creating a crispy crunchy coating. It is worth the effort as once cooked it feels like such an incredible treat.

Hint: Leftovers can easily be frozen and reheated in the oven.

INGREDIENTS

BATTER

1¼ cup cassava flour (you may require slightly more or less depending on your brand of flour)

1 ¼ cups tapioca starch

2 cups fizzy water

¼ tsp salt

CASSAVA CHIPS

1 cassava root peeled and cut into thick chips

5–10 TBSP light olive oil

FISH

3 large cod loins cut into 3 inch length pieces (9 pieces).

2 tsp garlic powder

¼ tsp salt

Enough light olive oil to deep fry the fish

COOKING STEPS

1 Preheat your oven to 220°C (fan).

BATTER

2 Mix the cassava flour, tapioca starch and salt together and add the fizzy water gradually, (you may not need it all). The mixture should look similar to a thick pancake mix.

CASSAVA CHIPS

3 Peel and cut the cassava root into thick chips, taking care to remove the hard fibrous core. Wash thoroughly (two or three times).

4 Boil the chips for 15 to 25 minutes (depending on your thickness) or until the cassava chips have softened and are cooked. (If you are able to pierce the chip easily with a small knife it is cooked). Drain and transfer to a large bowl.

5 Coat the chips in olive oil and cook in the oven for 25 minutes at 220°C until golden and crispy.

FISH

6 Heat the light olive oil in a small saucepan that is a suitable size to fry your fish.

7 Dry the cod loins with kitchen paper and cut into 3 inch length pieces and season with salt and garlic powder on both sides.

8 In batches coat the fish in batter and fry in olive oil for 5 to 7 minutes, taking care not to overload your pan. Turn the fish halfway through cooking, until it has a crispy golden coating.

FISH TACOS

MEDIUM
PREP: 15 MINUTES
COOKING: 60 MINUTES
SERVES 4
LARGE SHALLOW FRYING PAN & STERILISED JAR

INGREDIENTS

PICKLE

6 radishes thinly sliced

1 red onion thinly sliced

½ cup water boiled and cooled

½ cup apple cider vinegar

½ TBSP salt

TACOS (MAKES 8)

3 cups cassava flour

¼ tsp salt

½ TBSP onion powder

1 TBSP garlic powder

⅛ tsp turmeric powder

1 TBSP olive oil

Up to 2 cups boiling water added gradually

FISH

⅛ tsp turmeric powder

¼ cup cassava flour

½ tsp salt

½ TBSP garlic powder

½ TBSP onion powder

6 white fish fillets cut into strips

2 TBSP fresh coriander leaves to serve

1 lime quartered to serve

SALSA

Refer to Kiana's Mango Salsa recipe for ingredients

COOKING STEPS

PICKLE

1 Sterilise a jar large enough to fit your chopped radish and sliced onions. Once the jar has cooled, place your radish and onions at the bottom and cover with even quantities of cooled boiled water and apple cider vinegar, mixed with salt. Leave to marinate until the dish is ready to plate up.

TACOS

2 In a large bowl combine the cassava flour with the salt, onion, garlic and turmeric powders before adding the olive oil and mixing. Add boiling water gradually and mix thoroughly with a spatula. (You may need more or less boiling water depending on your brand of cassava flour). You are looking for a consistency where the dough easily forms a ball and leaves the bowl clean when mixed with the spatula. Add more flour if the dough is too sticky or more water if too dry.

3 Divide the dough into small balls depending on the size you would like your tacos, also bearing in mind the size of your pan. Cover the bowl with a tea towel to prevent the dough from drying out. Roll out each ball of dough between two sheets of baking paper into a circular shape, aiming for an even thickness of approximately 2 to 3 mm before cooking.

4 Heat the pan and cook on a medium to high heat for 1 to 2 minutes until little air bubbles appear on the surface. Once this happens turn the taco over and lightly press on the edges, or any uncooked areas with a spatula. Using the spatula or your hand, gently turn the taco in circular motions on both sides until cooked and if you are lucky it will inflate.

5 Place the cooked tacos on a metal cooling rack or a sheet of baking paper to cool slightly. I like to store mine in an airtight container, with small layers of baking paper between each taco to prevent them from sticking.

FISH

6 Mix the dry ingredients together in a bowl. Cut the fish fillets into even strips and coat in the seasoned cassava flour mix. Fry in olive oil on a medium heat for 2 minutes on each side until golden.

SALSA

7 Refer to Kiana's Mango Salsa recipe for method.

ASSEMBLY

8 Once all of your elements are ready, fill your taco with salsa, top with fish, some of your pickled radish and onion, fresh coriander and a squeeze of fresh lime. Fold the bottom of the taco up, creating an envelope for your beautiful ingredients so they don't escape. Serve and enjoy.

This is a real treat and one of my favourite dishes to eat as they hit your tastebuds with the sweet and tangy salsa, sharp and crunchy pickle and crispy fish.

Hints: You may require slightly more or less cassava flour depending on your brand. You can use any filleted fish to make this recipe. I used sea bream as it is so easy to pan fry. The tacos usually keep in the fridge for 3 to 4 days and can be reheated in a pan to soften.

—Sue

SALADS

THAI SALAD

EASY
PREP: 25 MINUTES
SERVES 4
JULIENNE PEELER OR MANDOLINE, GRATER & BLENDER

This salad reminds me of the wonderful taste of Thailand and is so refreshing and tangy. It works particularly well with grilled fish, prawns or chicken or is delicious on its own, topped with crispy fried shallots.

For the family add slices of ripe tomatoes and sliced green beans and top with crushed roasted peanuts for an added crunch.

Hint: If you aren't eating this salad straight away, refrigerate separately from the dressing and mix together before serving. —*Sue*

INGREDIENTS

2 medium carrots peeled and finely shredded

½ large cucumber core removed, finely sliced lengthways

125g asparagus cooked al dente and finely sliced lengthways

⅓ Chinese cabbage (napa), base section finely sliced

8 radishes finely sliced into thin strips

1 red onion finely sliced

3 TBSP fresh coriander finely chopped

3 TBSP fresh mint finely chopped

DRESSING

3 garlic cloves finely chopped

1 ½ TBSP fresh ginger finely chopped

3 TBSP fish sauce or 4 anchovy fillets finely chopped

2 limes zested and juiced

3 tsp coconut sugar

STEPS

1 Prepare all of your salad ingredients by finely slicing, shredding and chopping and combine in a large bowl.

2 Add your dressing ingredients to your blender and blitz to combine.'

3 Add your dressing to your salad, mix thoroughly and serve immediately.

SPINACH & ROCKET SALAD

EASY

5 to 10 MINUTES

SERVES 2

BLENDER

This light, zesty salad can be served with any fish or meat. It works particularly well with tinned sardines, mackerel or tuna and is so quick to prepare.

Hint: Pour over the dressing just before serving to keep it as fresh as possible. I only used 4 tablespoons of the dressing to prepare this salad for two people.

The dressing recipe makes approximately 8 tablespoons in total so the remainder can be stored in the fridge for another day.

INGREDIENTS

6 radishes quartered

1 avocado finely sliced

60g baby spinach

40g rocket leaves

DRESSING

1 lemon juiced (2 TBSP)

6 TBSP olive oil

2 TBSP shallots chopped

½ TBSP honey

1 tsp garlic powder

Salt to taste

STEPS

1. Quarter the radishes. Cut the avocados in half and carefully remove stone.
2. Scoop out the flesh with a spoon, finely slice and set aside.
3. Cut the lemon in half and squeeze the juice into a small bowl. Remove the seeds, decant the juice into a blender and add the olive oil, chopped shallots, honey, garlic powder and salt. Blitz until smooth.
4. Combine the leaves and radishes and pour over the dressing. Mix well and then add the avocado. Serve immediately.

CHINESE CABBAGE COLESLAW

EASY

PREP: 20 MINUTES

SERVES 10

FOOD PROCESSOR, GRATER, HAND BLENDER

This recipe makes a delicious breakfast or lunch and lasts for several days in the fridge in an airtight container. It is best to just take out what you need and add some of the dressing when you are ready to eat.

Hint: This works well with grilled sardines and you can also use tinned tuna, mackerel, leftover chicken, duck or salmon.

INGREDIENTS

1 Chinese (napa) cabbage finely shredded

1 cup grated radish

1 cup grated carrot

½ red onion thinly sliced

½ cup chopped fresh parsley (you can substitute coriander leaf)

Salt to taste

1 tin of sardines, tuna or mackerel

DRESSING

1 ripe avocado (peeled and pitted)

⅓ cup avocado oil (or extra-virgin olive oil)

2 limes juiced

2 tsp apple cider vinegar

Salt to taste

2 drops food grade lime essential oil – optional

Extra water if dressing is too thick

STEPS

1. In a large bowl, mix together the cabbage, radish, carrot, onion, parsley and salt.
2. Place all the dressing ingredients into a hand blender and blitz until smooth. Add extra water a tablespoon at a time if the mixture is too thick.
3. Store the dressing separately in an airtight container in the fridge until you are ready to use. The lime will stop the avocado from browning and it should last several days.
4. When ready to eat, place a portion size of salad into a bowl with 2–3 tablespoons of dressing. Mix well to combine. Create a pile of coleslaw on a plate. Top with sardines, tuna, mackerel or other fish or meat protein.

STRAWBERRY & ROCKET SALAD

EASY

PREP: 5 to 10 MINUTES

SERVES 2

JAR WITH LID

This super simple salad is nutrient dense and pairs well with fish, chicken or steak.

INGREDIENTS

½ avocado peeled and diced

5 cm slice of cucumber diced

5–6 strawberries diced

2 cups fresh rocket leaves

DRESSING

3 TBSP avocado oil

1 TBSP apple cider vinegar

½ lime juiced

1 tsp chopped shallots

Salt to taste

STEPS

1. Peel and pit your avocado and dice into cubes. Peel your cucumber and dice along with your strawberries and place into a bowl. Add the rocket leaves and mix well.
2. Put all the dressing ingredients into the jar, pop the lid on firmly and give it a good shake.
3. Add 1–2 TBSP of dressing to the salad to your taste, mix well and serve immediately. Extra dressing can be stored in the jam jar to be used later.

KIANA'S MANGO SALSA

EASY
PREP: 15 MINUTES
SERVES 4
JAR WITH LID

My daughter loves mango and helped to create the recipe for this irresistible salsa. This dish is sweet and savoury, simple to make and incredibly refreshing. It is perfect with fish and is so colourful that it's enough to brighten anyone's day.

Hint: Try to use a mango that is ripe but not too soft as it will be tricky to cut into cubes. I found that using frozen mango also works well too.

—Sue

INGREDIENTS

SALSA

1 large mango peeled, pitted and finely diced

1 large avocado peeled, pitted and finely diced

2 shallots finely diced

1 cup cucumber peeled and finely diced (core removed)

1 kiwi peeled and finely chopped

9 radishes finely chopped

½ cup fresh coriander leaves chopped

¼ cup fresh mint leaves chopped

DRESSING

1 garlic clove grated

1 TBSP olive oil

Zest of 1 lime (or one drop of food grade lime essential oil)

1 lime juiced

Salt to taste

STEPS

1. Prepare all of the salsa ingredients and combine in a large bowl.
2. Place all the dressing ingredients into a clean jam jar. Secure the lid and shake to combine. Pour over the salsa and mix well.
3. This will keep in an airtight container in the fridge for several days.

MIXED LEAVES, ASPARAGUS & PINEAPPLE SALAD

EASY
PREP: 10 MINUTES
SERVES 2
SAUCEPAN OR STEAMER

This salad is quick, easy and versatile and is delicious with most dishes, especially fish, pâté and Thai-inspired main courses.

Hint: This dressing recipe makes 8 TBSPs. Just use 1–2 TBSPs to suit your palate and store the remainder in an airtight container for another dish.

INGREDIENTS

1 small handful of fresh asparagus, chopped into 3 cm lengths

1 small head of romaine lettuce, roughly torn

1 large handful of baby leaf spinach

8–10 fresh sweet basil leaves, roughly torn

½ cup chopped pineapple (fresh or tinned)

DRESSING

6 TBSP olive oil

2 TBSP red wine vinegar

Salt to taste

STEPS

1. Lightly cook the asparagus in a pan of boiling water (or steam) whilst you are preparing everything else (approx. 5 minutes).
2. In a large bowl combine all the leaves and the chopped pineapple.
3. When making a quick salad dressing a great tip is to use an old jam jar which has been cleaned thoroughly. Put all the dressing ingredients into the jam jar, pop the lid on firmly and give it a good shake. (Any leftover dressing can then be stored in the jar for another day.)
4. Once the asparagus is cooked, drain and run under cold water. Pat dry with some kitchen roll and add to the leaves, along with the dressing and mix together thoroughly.
5. Serve and enjoy.

BEETROOT SALAD

EASY
PREP: 10 MINUTES
COOKING: 20 to 40 MINUTES
SERVES 2
LARGE SAUCEPAN

This is a great little salad and will store for several days in an air-tight container in the fridge. It can be enjoyed by itself, with fish, chicken or Moroccan lamb, or can be added to other salads.

Hint: Once you have reintroduced some spices, you can add a little black pepper and ½ tsp ground cumin for a more Moroccan flavour.

INGREDIENTS

1 tsp sea salt

4 medium sized beetroots with leaves still attached

1 red onion, thinly sliced

2–3 TBSP fresh curly leaf parsley, chopped

DRESSING

Juice of 1 lemon

2 garlic cloves, minced

4 TBSP extra virgin olive oil

Salt to taste

COOKING STEPS

1 Bring a large pot of salted water to the boil. Meanwhile, wash the beetroots and trim the leaves leaving 2–3 cm of the stalks still attached to the beetroot (this will stop the colour bleeding out of the roots). Don't throw away the leaves - you can use those in the Sautéed Beet Greens recipe another day.

2 Add the beetroots to the boiling water and cook on a medium heat for 20–40 minutes, (cooking time will depend on the size of the beetroot). Test with a knife and once they are soft, drain and leave to cool for a few minutes until safe to handle.

3 Cool the beetroots further under running cold water as you rub off the skins with your fingers. (You may want to use rubber gloves to avoid staining your hands).

4 Once the skin has been removed, slice off the top and bottom of each beetroot, cut into segments, like an orange and place in a bowl with the red onion and parsley.

DRESSING

5 In a bowl, whisk together the lemon, garlic, olive oil and salt to taste. Drizzle the dressing over the beetroots, adding the quantity of dressing to your taste and mix well. Serve and enjoy. Any remaining dressing can be stored in an air-tight container in the fridge.

KILO

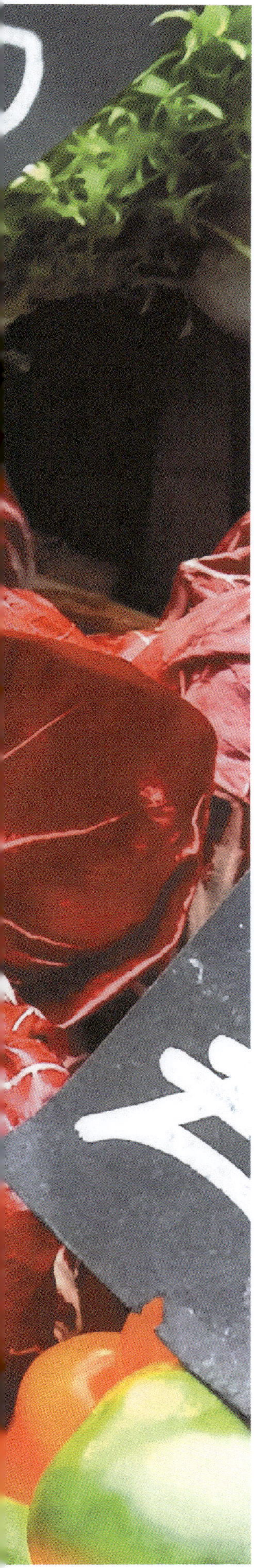

VEGETABLES

GREEN CABBAGE WITH LEEKS

EASY

PREP: 10 MINUTES
COOKING: 20 MINUTES

SERVES 4

FRYING PAN OR WOK

The cruciferous family of vegetables (cabbage, broccoli, cauliflower and brussel sprouts) are very nutrient dense and I try to include at least one of them every day. —*Claire*

Hint: You can switch the leeks for onions and experiment with different herbs. It is ideal to cook in advance and warm up when ready and it stores well, so it lends itself to batch cooking. A great addition to breakfast or throw some into bone broth for a more hearty breakfast soup.

INGREDIENTS

1 small green cabbage shredded

1 leek sliced

2 TBSP olive oil

1 tsp dried sage, or a handful of fresh chopped sage leaves

Salt to taste

COOKING STEPS

1 Heat the oil in a wok or large frying pan and add the leeks. Stir until the leeks become translucent, about 3 minutes.

2 Throw in the cabbage and stir to mix in the leeks. Continue to cook for a few minutes until the cabbage seems to soften a little. Add the sage and salt to taste.

3 Lower the temperature and cover with a lid and cook for a further 10 minutes, stirring occasionally so it doesn't stick. Serve and enjoy.

RED CABBAGE

EASY
PREP: 10 MINUTES
COOKING: 20 MINUTES
SERVES 4
FRYING PAN OR WOK

I love red cabbage and used to make it in the oven with butter and vinegar and it took almost two hours. This one is just as delicious and only needs to cook for 20 minutes. It stores well in the fridge and is simply fabulous with meat patties and avocado for breakfast, so make plenty! You can make this in advance and warm it up when the rest of the meal is ready and it stores and freezes well, so it lends itself to batch cooking. —*Claire*

Hint: As another option you may like to throw in some chopped apple or raisins. I like to pair it with duck in orange sauce, roast chicken, pork or a hearty casserole.

Hint: Once you have introduced some spices back into your diet, you can add 1 TBSP whole black mustard seeds at the same time you add the maple syrup.

INGREDIENTS

1 small red cabbage shredded

1 small red onion thinly sliced

2 TBSP olive oil

¼ cup organic apple cider vinegar

2 TBSP maple syrup

Salt to taste

COOKING STEPS

1. Heat the oil in a wok and add the onion. Stir until the onion becomes translucent, cooking for approximately 3 minutes.
2. Throw in the cabbage and stir well. Continue to mix for a few minutes until the cabbage softens a little, approximately 5 minutes.
3. Add the apple cider vinegar and maple syrup and mix well. The cabbage will change from purple to deep pink at this point.
4. Add salt to taste and lower the temperature and cook for a further 10 minutes, stirring occasionally so it doesn't stick.

STIR FRIED PAK CHOI

EASY

PREP: 5 MINUTES
COOKING: 5 MINUTES

SERVES 4

FRYING PAN OR WOK

Pak choi is one of my favourite green vegetables as it is so quick to cook and there is very little preparation required. It is a member of the cabbage family and has many names including pak choi, bok choy, horse's ear, Chinese celery cabbage and white mustard cabbage. It can be served as a tempting side dish and is particularly good with fish or can easily be wilted into piping hot bone broth. This dish takes just 10 minutes to prepare and cook and is full of flavour.

Hint: Pak choi is best served with a little crunch, so once the darker green leaves have wilted it is ready to serve.

INGREDIENTS

2 TBSP olive or avocado oil

1 TBSP ginger chopped

2 shallots thinly sliced

2 large cloves garlic chopped

4 pak choi quartered

2 TBSP coconut aminos

1 TBSP fish sauce

Small handful of fresh coriander (optional)

COOKING STEPS

1. Heat the oil in a wok, add the ginger and shallots and fry for 2 to 3 minutes on a medium to high heat until lightly golden in colour. Reduce the heat to a low simmer and add in the garlic, stirring continuously.
2. Wash and dry the pak choi, cut into quarters and add to the pan with coconut aminos and fish sauce. Stir well and cook on a medium heat for 3 to 5 minutes until the pak choi has softened slightly.
3. When the darker green leaves have wilted and the lighter stalks have softened slightly, remove from the heat. Stir in chopped coriander and serve immediately.

GINGER & GARLIC KALE

EASY

PREP: 10 MINUTES
COOKING: 10 to 15 MINUTES

SERVES 4

FRYING PAN OR WOK

Cavolo nero is a type of kale that is native to the Mediterranean coast and is also known as Tuscan kale, lacinato, dinosaur kale, and black cabbage.

Hint: To cook evenly it is best to remove the central stems before chopping the leaves, as they can be tough and chewy. It stores well in the fridge for 3 to 4 days and also freezes well for up to a month.

An alternative recipe would be to remove the ginger and add the zest of one lemon before serving.

INGREDIENTS

2 TBSP olive oil

4 garlic cloves finely chopped

1 TBSP ginger finely chopped

200 g cavolo nero, stems removed and finely chopped

2 tsp garlic powder

2 TBSP water

Salt to taste

COOKING STEPS

1. Add the olive oil to the pan. On a low heat fry the garlic and ginger for 3 to 4 minutes until softened, taking care not to brown the garlic.
2. Turn up the heat slightly and add the cavolo nero, garlic powder, water and salt, stirring well. Cover with a lid, stirring occasionally, adding more water if required.
3. Cook for approximately 10 to 15 minutes until the cavolo nero is tender and the water has evaporated. Remove from the heat, serve and enjoy.

HONEY & THYME ROASTED PARSNIPS

EASY
PREP: 5 MINUTES
COOKING: 40 MINUTES
SERVES 4
ROASTING TIN

These parsnips have just the right amount of sweet and savoury to make them an extremely moreish side dish. They are so quick to prepare, roast beautifully in the oven, turning golden and crispy and the whole-roasted garlic cloves are an additional treat.

Hint: As another option you may like to roast your parsnips with some carrots to save time as this recipe works beautifully. These are very handy to keep in the freezer and heat up as required.

INGREDIENTS

500g parsnips

2 TBSP olive or avocado oil

Salt to taste

1 TBSP fresh thyme

1 TBSP garlic powder

1 TBSP honey

6 cloves garlic (unpeeled)

COOKING STEPS

1. Preheat your oven to 170°C. Peel, top and tail your parsnips, removing the inner core if particularly hard and cutting them into even sizes.
2. Place in a large saucepan, cover with salted water and bring to the boil and cook for 5 minutes. Drain in a colander and leave to steam-dry for 2 minutes.
3. Place the parsnips in a roasting tray, drizzle with oil and gently mix to coat evenly. Sprinkle with salt, thyme, garlic powder and honey and gently toss to coat.
4. Roast for 40 mins, turning halfway. Add in the cloves of garlic to roast for the last 15 minutes of cooking time until the parsnips are golden brown.

ORANGE & GINGER GLAZED CARROTS

EASY

PREP: 5 MINUTES
COOKING: 35 MINUTES

SERVES 4

GRATER & ROASTING TIN

These carrots are made with a touch of warming ginger and fresh orange zest, making them a perfectly roasted side dish. They practically take care of themselves in the oven and are super simple to prepare.

Hint: This recipe also works well with large chunks of butternut squash and is so handy to keep in the freezer and heat up on days when you are pushed for time.

INGREDIENTS

500g carrots

2 TBSP olive or avocado oil

1 TBSP ginger grated

1 orange zested and juiced

1 TBSP fresh thyme

1 TBSP garlic powder

Salt to taste

COOKING STEPS

1. Preheat your oven to 170°C (fan).
2. Peel, top and tail your carrots, cutting them into even sizes.
3. Place the carrots in a roasting tray, drizzle with oil and gently mix to coat evenly. Sprinkle with ginger, orange zest and juice, thyme, garlic powder and salt. Mix thoroughly so that the carrots are coated well.
4. Roast for 35 mins, turning halfway until the carrots are glazed and slightly caramelised.

SAUTÉED BEET GREENS

EASY
PREP: 10 MINUTES
COOKING: 10 MINUTES
SERVES 2
FRYING PAN OR WOK

When you cook beetroots, don't throw away the green leaves since they are highly nutritious! This is my favourite way to cook them. —*Claire*

INGREDIENTS

1–2 TBSP olive oil

3 shallots (or ½ a small onion) diced

2 cloves garlic finely chopped

1 bunch of beetroot leaves chopped

Salt to taste

COOKING STEPS

1. Heat the oil in a pan over a medium heat. Add the shallots and garlic and cook until translucent.
2. Meanwhile, chop the beet greens and tender stems and add to the pan.
3. Add a twist of salt and cook until tender—super easy!

FERMENTED FOODS, SAUCES & GRAVY

SUPER-SIMPLE SAUERKRAUT

EASY

PREP: 10 MINUTES
FERMENTATION: 3 to 10 DAYS

SERVES 20

WIDE-NECKED GLASS MASON JAR, SMALL JAR TO FIT INSIDE MASON JAR

This is one of the easiest homemade fermented foods to make. It's delicious, better than anything you'll buy, super-sour and packed full of beneficial gut bacteria, thanks to the presence of lactobacillus on the leaves which are responsible for the fermentation process and so many great uses in your gut. Simply add a tablespoon as a condiment with salad, homemade burgers, steak, anything really. You can even throw some into your morning bone broth with some leftover chicken, grated ginger and spring onion—scrumptious! —*Claire*

INGREDIENTS

1 whole green, white or red cabbage

2 TBSP sea salt

COOKING STEPS

1 Rinse the mason jar with very warm water and then hot water from a recently boiled kettle. You want to sterilise it but not cause it to crack. Also give the outside of the jam jar a good wash—we want everything as clean as possible so we only get the good bacteria. Wash your hands thoroughly as you'll be using them to massage the cabbage. Peel off the thick outer cabbage leaves and keep to one side for later.

2 Cut the cabbage into quarters down the central stalk, take out the hard stalk and discard. Finely shred the cabbage in a food processor or using a large sharp knife (make sure all your equipment has been rinsed in boiling water before using it). Place in a large mixing bowl and cover with the salt. Start to combine the cabbage and salt by massaging and squeezing. It will very quickly get wet and limp—this takes about 5–10 minutes.

3 Grab the limp cabbage and pack it into the mason jar, tapping it down firmly either with your fist or the jam jar, pour any liquid released from massaging the cabbage into the mason jar as well. Squeeze as much of the air out as possible—there will be a layer of water at the top at this point. Cover the surface with one of the discarded outer cabbage leaves to keep the shredded cabbage underwater.

4 Cover the jar either with a muslin cloth and elastic band or with the mason jar lid. Over the next 3–10 days bubbles will be released. If you seal the mason jar with the lid, remove the lid to release the gases each day and press the cabbage down deeper to submerge it. Once it stops creating gas, it's ready to eat.

5 The taste will evolve with time. When it is to your taste (3–10 days) you can remove the large cabbage leaf covering the sauerkraut, pop the lid on and store in the fridge. It's edible at any time so just go with your taste buds. Once you have reintroduced seeds, you can add 1 TBSP caraway seeds or juniper berries at stage 3 for added flavour.

AIP-INSPIRED KIMCHI

EASY
PREP: 20 MINUTES
BRINING & ASSEMBLY: 2 HOURS 10 MINUTES
FERMENTATION: 2 to 3 DAYS
2 LARGE JARS
JULIENNE PEELER OR MANDOLINE, BLENDER & 2 LARGE STERILISED JARS

This is an AIP inspired Kimchi, without the fiery Korean spice. It is still full of flavour and also good for you due to the fermentation process that generates good bacteria, making this an excellent probiotic.

Hint: The kimchi keeps in the fridge for up to one month (if it lasts that long) and will become more flavoursome the longer it ferments.

INGREDIENTS

1 Chinese cabbage (napa)

4 TBSP sea salt

1 large bowl of water

10 garlic cloves chopped

1 TBSP ginger

4 TBSP fish sauce

1 TBSP maple syrup

1 TBSP apple cider vinegar

7 radishes cut into matchsticks

1 carrot shredded

6 spring onions finely sliced

Up to 2 cups reserved brine water

COOKING STEPS

1. Wash your hands thoroughly as you'll be using them to massage the cabbage. Quarter the cabbage and cut into 3 cm strips. Place into a large mixing bowl, wash thoroughly and drain. Place the washed cabbage back into the mixing bowl with 4 TBSP sea salt, massaging the salt into the cabbage using your hands. Cover with cold water and place a plate on top to keep the cabbage submerged in the brine. Set aside for 2 hours.
2. Meanwhile blend the garlic, ginger and fish sauce, maple syrup and apple cider vinegar until smooth and set aside.
3. After 2 hours drain the brine, reserving it for later. Rinse the cabbage thoroughly with cold water and squeeze out any excess moisture. Place the cabbage into a large bowl, add the blended ingredients, radish and spring onions, coating all of the vegetables by mixing thoroughly.
4. Spoon the mixture into a large sterilised jar or two depending on the size you have. Taking care to leave a 2 cm gap at the top of the jar, press the vegetables down to compact them. Add some of the reserved brine so the vegetables are submerged under the juices and place the lid on. Leave at room temperature to ferment for 2 to 3 days, opening each day to ensure all of the vegetables are still fully submerged in the brine and to release any gases. You can consume straight away but after 2 to 3 days the kimchi should develop in flavour at which point you can refrigerate.

HOMEMADE KETCHUP

EASY

PREP: 10 MINUTES
COOKING: 30 MINUTES

SERVES 4

SAUCEPAN & BLENDER

Delicious as a dip or can be used to make a tasty cooking sauce.

INGREDIENTS

½ cup tamarind pulp

200ml boiling water

¼ tsp salt

1 cup + 1 TBSP frozen dark sweet cherries pitted

⅓ cup cooked beetroot

1 tsp organic apple cider vinegar

¼ cup coconut sugar

5 garlic cloves roughly chopped

2 tsp tapioca starch (as necessary)

1 TBSP cold water (as necessary)

COOKING STEPS

1. Place the tamarind pulp in a saucepan with the boiling water and simmer with the lid on a medium heat for 5 minutes, stirring occasionally. Remove any seeds and strain into a bowl using a sieve. Push the pulp through the sieve with a spoon and scrape the underside of the sieve with a spatula to collect the as much of the tamarind liquid as possible.
2. Transfer the sieved tamarind liquid back into the saucepan and add the salt, cherries, beetroot, cider vinegar and coconut sugar, keeping the pan on simmer with the lid on for a further 10 minutes until cooked.
3. Meanwhile peel and roughly chop the garlic and add to the pan, cooking for 2 to 3 minutes. Decant the cooked mixture into a blender and whiz into a smooth puree. If you would like to thicken your puree to a ketchup like consistency, transfer the mixture back to the saucepan.
4. Mix the tapioca starch and water together thoroughly and pour into the sauce, stirring well until thickened to the desired consistency.
5. Transfer every last mouth-watering drop to a storage jar and enjoy with chips or nachos.

BARBEQUE SAUCE

EASY

PREP: 15 MINUTES
COOKING: 30 MINUTES

12 to 13 TBSP

SAUCEPAN, HAND BLENDER OR FOOD PROCESSOR

This sauce is incredibly moreish and works well as a dip. It can be used as a marinade and also for adding a little extra flavour to baste meat during cooking. It is smoky, sweet, sticky and tangy and caramelises beautifully.

Hint: Smoked sea salt works particularly well in this dish adding a hint of BBQ smokiness.

INGREDIENTS

3 TBSP olive oil

1 medium onion chopped

1 ½ TBSP ginger chopped

5 cloves garlic chopped

½ cup plums peeled and chopped

½ cup nectarines peeled and chopped

2 tsp fresh rosemary

2 tsp fresh thyme

2 tsp fresh tarragon

½ cup water

½ TBSP onion powder

1 TBSP garlic powder

½ cup honey

2 TBSP coconut aminos

2 TBSP apple cider vinegar

Salt to taste

COOKING STEPS

1. Heat the olive oil in a saucepan, add the onions and ginger and place the lid on the saucepan. Simmer on a low to medium heat for 10 minutes until the onions caramelise and are dark brown in colour, stirring occasionally.
2. Add the garlic and fry for 3 to 4 minutes until softened, before adding the chopped plums and nectarines. Place the lid on the saucepan and simmer for 4 to 5 minutes until softened, stirring occasionally.
3. Once the fruit has softened to a jam like consistency add the fresh herbs and mix well. Leave to simmer for 2 to 3 minutes with the lid on.
4. Remove the lid and add the water, onion and garlic powders, honey, coconut aminos and apple cider vinegar and stir to combine. Cook on a medium heat for 4 to 5 minutes until the consistency has thickened slightly.
5. Using a hand blender or food processor blitz into a smooth sauce. Add salt to taste, (preferably smoked sea salt if you have this available) and stir to combine.

TAMARIND SAUCE

EASY

PREP: 15 MINUTES
COOKING: 30 MINUTES

APPROX. 900 ML

SAUCEPAN & BLENDER

This tamarind sauce is so versatile and can be used as a marinade, cooking or dipping sauce or dressing. It has a sweet and sour taste and is perfect served with curry or Thai larb. It even works in shepherd's pie!

Hint: The sauce can be made in a large batch as it is great for freezing in ice cube trays and defrosting as needed.

INGREDIENTS

400g tamarind pulp (including seeds)

2 cups boiling water

2 TBSP olive oil

3 shallots chopped

2 TBSP ginger chopped

6 garlic cloves chopped

1 ripe mango peeled and cubed (1 cup)

Up to ½ cup water

¾ cup maple syrup

2 TBSP garlic powder

½ TBSP salt

Up to ¼ cup water (if required)

COOKING STEPS

1. Place the tamarind pulp in a saucepan with the boiling water and simmer on a medium heat with the lid on for 5 minutes, stirring occasionally. Remove any seeds and strain into a bowl using a sieve, (you may have to do this in a couple of batches). Push the pulp through the sieve with a spoon and scrape the underside of the sieve with a spatula to collect the as much of the liquid as possible. You should end up with approximately 2 cups of sauce after this stage.
2. Using the same saucepan cook the shallots and ginger for 2 to 3 minutes until softened. Add the garlic and cook for a further 2 minutes until fragrant. At this point add the mango and ½ cup water and cook with the lid on for 4 to 5 minutes until a soft jam like consistency is achieved.
3. Next add the maple syrup, garlic powder, salt and your sieved tamarind sauce and cook with the lid off for 4 to 5 minutes to let all of the flavours combine.
4. Decant the cooked mixture into a blender and whiz into a smooth puree. You should at this stage be able to see if the desired 'ketchup-like' consistency has been achieved. If not transfer the mixture back to the saucepan and add a little water if you would like to loosen your sauce and mix well.
5. If your sauce requires thickening leave on a gentle heat for up to 5 minutes to thicken slightly.
6. Transfer every last mouth-watering drop to a jar. Serve and enjoy.

CHEESE SAUCE

EASY

PREP: 5 MINUTES
COOKING: 15 MINUTES

APPROX. 350 ML

SAUCEPAN & WHISK

This cheese sauce can be added into sweet potato mash, used to make cauliflower cheese or enjoyed with nachos. It is super simple to make and makes a great alternative to dairy.

Hint: The sauce will thicken if placed in the fridge overnight but can be easily reheated in a saucepan with a few drops of water to regain the desired consistency.

INGREDIENTS

1 cup coconut milk

½ tsp salt

2 TBSP extra virgin olive oil

5 tsp nutritional yeast

1 to 2 tsp apple cider vinegar (depending on personal taste)

¼ tsp turmeric powder

1 tsp onion powder

1 tsp garlic powder

¼ cup tapioca starch

Up to 1 cup of water (depending on desired consistency)

COOKING STEPS

1. In a cold saucepan add coconut milk, salt, olive oil, nutritional yeast, apple cider vinegar, turmeric, onion and garlic powders and tapioca starch and whisk until all of the ingredients are fully combined.
2. Turn on the heat and cook on a medium to low heat for 3 to 5 minutes, whisking continuously until the until the tapioca starch is cooked and the sauce thickens.
3. Depending on the thickness of the sauce you would like to achieve add a little water to loosen. Lower the heat and continue whisking for a further 3 to 5 minutes until the desired consistency is achieved.
4. Remove from heat and decant into a bowl to prevent the sauce from cooking further.

NEIL'S GRAVY

EASY
PREP: 10 MINUTES
COOKING: 5 MINUTES AFTER CHICKEN IS COOKED
SERVES 4
WIRE RACK & ROASTING TIN

This perfectly flavoured gravy is made by utilising precious meat juices and bone broth for a rich, smooth and beautifully flavoured sauce. My job growing up was to make the gravy and the custard and so I have a great fondness for gravy. When homemade gravy is this quick and delicious, I guarantee the family will never want granules ever again.

Gravy conjures up feeling of being home, being safe and being nourished. My husband Neil certainly knows the way to my heart with this recipe—enjoy! —*Claire*

Hint: To adjust the thickness of your gravy add more hot water if it is too thick or more arrowroot mixed with water to thicken. An alternative can be made in a saucepan in a hurry but the flavour won't be as rich.

You can also make this gravy under a roast beef joint which is also delicious.

INGREDIENTS

1 whole raw chicken

¼ onion diced

2-3 mushroom diced

1 rasher of unsmoked bacon finely chopped

1 TBSP coconut aminos

½ cup home-made bone broth or ½ cup water

2 tsp arrowroot powder mixed with 2 TBSP of water

Salt to taste

COOKING STEPS

1. Preheat your oven to 180°C (fan).
2. Place the roasting tin on the stove over a medium heat and add the diced onion, sliced mushrooms and diced bacon. Fry for 5 minutes or until golden brown in colour, stirring well.
3. Add the coconut aminos and home-made bone broth (water can be used if there is no broth available but it will affect the flavour).
4. Place your roasting chicken on a wire rack over the gravy base in the roasting tin.
5. Cook your chicken in the oven according to weight guidelines. Once your chicken is cooked remove it from the oven and leave to rest.
6. Place your roasting tin onto your stove and with a wooden spatula loosen the meat juices. You may find that some of these may have hardened and are now dark in colour. Do not discard these, they provide precious flavour and colour.
7. Stir well and if the liquid has dried out add more bone broth or water until you have sufficient liquid for your gravy.
8. Mix the arrowroot powder with the water until smooth and add to the roasting tin. Stir continuously as the arrowroot powder cooks.
9. After a few minutes the gravy should lose its cloudy appearance. Season with salt and serve hot. If you are not fond of "bits" in your gravy, simply sieve the finished gravy, pressing every last scrumptious drop through the mesh with a spoon.

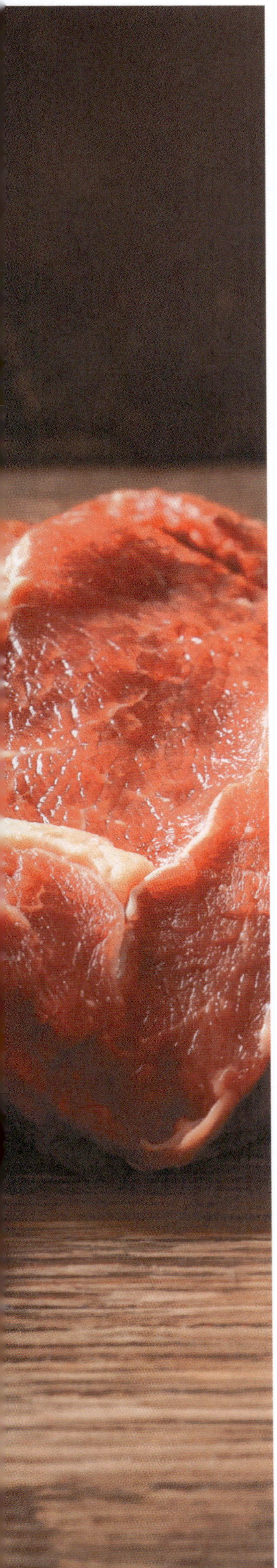

POULTRY & MEAT

BAKED CRISPY CHICKEN WINGS WITH A TANGY ORANGE SAUCE

MEDIUM

PREP: 20 MINUTES
COOKING: 40 MINUTES

SERVES 4

WIRE RACK & SAUCEPAN

These chicken wings are so moreish and can be enjoyed on their own or with a tangy orange sauce.

They really are finger-licking good!

INGREDIENTS

CRISPY CHICKEN WINGS

1kg chicken wings

1 TBSP olive oil

8 to 10 TBSP cassava flour (you may require slightly more or less depending on your brand of flour)

1 tsp pink Himalayan salt

3 TBSP garlic powder

2 TBSP ginger powder

3 TBSP onion powder

Handful of chopped coriander to finish the dish

TANGY ORANGE SAUCE

1/3 cup freshly squeezed orange juice

2 TBSP maple syrup

1 tsp honey

¼ cup coconut aminos

1 TBSP chopped garlic

2 tsp chopped ginger

¼ tsp salt

2 tsp tapioca starch mixed with 2 tsp cold water

½ cup chopped spring onion

COOKING STEPS

1 Preheat your oven to 230°C (fan).

CRISPY CHICKEN WINGS

2 Place the chicken wings into a large bowl and drizzle with 1 TBSP olive oil before mixing.

3 Add sufficient cassava flour to coat the chicken wings thoroughly. Next add the salt and garlic, ginger and onion powders and mix thoroughly.

4 Place on a wire rack in the oven for approximately 40 minutes turning halfway through, until the chicken has a crispy golden coating.

TANGY ORANGE SAUCE

5 Mix all of the ingredients together leaving out the tapioca starch mixture and chopped spring onions.

6 Heat the liquid gently for 5 to 10 minutes, stirring occasionally.

7 Add the tapioca starch mixture and whisk until the sauce thickens, (usually approx. 2 minutes).

8 Stir in the chopped spring onions and enjoy as a dipping sauce on the side or drizzled over the crispy chicken wings.

9 Sprinkle over a handful of chopped coriander to finish the dish and serve and enjoy.

HONEY GLAZED CHICKEN

EASY

PREP: 10 MINUTES
COOKING: 20 MINUTES

SERVES 4 to 6

FRYING PAN OR WOK WITH LID

This dish uses only a few ingredients that transform into such a tasty, mouth-watering sauce, also suited to salmon, pork or prawns.

I love to serve it simply with pak choi and cauliflower rice.

Hint: To minimise the cooking time cut each chicken breast diagonally into two or three even slices, ensuring they are all roughly the same size to achieve an even cooking time.

INGREDIENTS

1kg chicken breast fillets, skinned

¼ tsp salt

½ cup cassava flour (you may require slightly more or less depending on your brand of flour)

5 TBSP olive oil

6 garlic cloves finely chopped

1 TBSP ginger

3 TBSP apple cider vinegar

2 TBSP coconut aminos

½ cup honey or maple syrup

1 TBSP fish sauce

4 spring onions finely chopped

COOKING STEPS

1. Cut your chicken breasts diagonally into 2 or 3 even slices, ensuring they are all roughly the same size. Sprinkle with ¼ tsp salt to season and ½ cup cassava flour, coating both sides.
2. Heat 4 TSBP olive oil in the pan or wok on a medium to high heat and fry the chicken for 2 to 3 minutes on each side until golden.
3. With the chicken still in the pan, turn the heat down slightly. Creating a little space in the pan or wok, add the remaining TBSP of olive oil and fry the ginger and garlic for approximately 4 minutes until fragrant.
4. Add the apple cider vinegar, coconut aminos, honey or maple syrup and fish sauce and shake the pan to combine. Place the lid on the pan and cook on a medium heat for 4 minutes, at which stage the sauce should bubble and turn a light golden brown. Turn the chicken over and cook for another 4 minutes with the lid on. Remove the lid and continue to cook for a further 2 minutes to thicken the sauce.
5. Sprinkle over the chopped spring onions and serve with plenty of sauce.

TENDER DUCK BREAST WITH AN ORANGE & ROSEMARY SAUCE

EASY
PREP: 5 MINUTES
COOKING: 15 MINUTES
RESTING: 10 MINUTES
SERVES 4
FRYING PAN & SAUCEPAN

Prepping hint: Ensure your duck breasts are thoroughly dry and bring them to room temperature before seasoning and cooking

Hint: Keep the duck fat in the pan, cool , decant into a glass container and refrigerate for brilliant roast sweet potatoes!

INGREDIENTS

DUCK

2 duck breasts (skin on)

Salt to taste

ORANGE AND ROSEMARY SAUCE

2 TBSP fresh rosemary chopped or 1 TBSP of dried rosemary

1 cup of 100% orange juice (or get busy squeezing)

2 TBSP maple syrup

COOKING STEPS

DUCK

1. Preheat your oven on to 200°C (fan) and place a baking tray in the centre to heat.
2. With a sharp knife, score the skin of the duck breast with parallel cuts 1 cm apart, taking care not to cut all the way to the flesh. Season well with salt and place in a cold frying pan, skin side down.
3. Turn the pan onto a medium heat to let the fat melt and the skin to crisp up. When you can see the duck fat melting and appearing in the pan, turn up the heat to create a skin that is golden and crisp. Adjust the temperature of your hob, taking care not to burn the skin.
4. Turn the duck breasts over briefly for a minute to seal the other side and then transfer the breasts to the preheated tray in the oven, skin side up for 6–8 minutes.
5. Remove duck breasts from oven and transfer to a plate. Allow to rest for 10 minutes before slicing. This is delicious with orange and rosemary sauce, mashed sweet potatoes and stir fried red cabbage, or eaten cold with a salad.

ORANGE AND ROSEMARY SAUCE

6. Place the rosemary, orange juice and maple syrup in the saucepan. Bring to boil and simmer gently with the lid on for about 20 minutes, stirring regularly.
7. Reduce the sauce to a thickness that suits you. I like it reduced until it starts to thicken and makes a sticky glaze when you pour it over the carved duck.

THAI LARB

EASY
PREP: 10 MINUTES
COOKING: 20 MINUTES
SERVES 4
WOK OR LARGE FRYING PAN & GRATER

This delightful version of Thai larb is a flavour filled salad served with a tangy tamarind and herb dressing, topped with fresh herbs, crunchy carrot and radishes.

Hint: Larb is a type of Asian meat salad and can be made with pork, turkey or chicken mince and served with lettuce cups or quite simply with baby spinach.

INGREDIENTS

2 TBSP avocado oil

500g turkey mince

1 ½ TBSP fish sauce

2 TBSP coconut aminos

3 kaffir lime leaves torn

2 TBSP avocado oil

2 shallots sliced

1 TBSP ginger grated

3 cloves garlic finely chopped

2 TBSP lemongrass finely chopped or blended

3 tsp coconut sugar

1 lime zested and juiced

3 TBSP fresh coriander chopped

3 TBSP fresh mint chopped

3 TBSP fresh Thai sweet basil chopped

1 handful of baby spinach leaves or lettuce cups

for serving

2 carrots shredded

4 radishes thinly sliced

TAMARIND SAUCE

Refer to Tamarind Sauce recipe for ingredients

HERB DRESSING

Refer to the Grilled Mackerel and Herb Dressing recipe for ingredients

COOKING STEPS

1. In a pan or a wok heat the avocado oil and fry the mince on a medium-high heat, breaking it into small pieces until it's fully cooked all the way through.
2. If using pork mince decant and reserve the oil separately. Add the fish sauce, coconut aminos and torn kaffir lime leaves. Cook for a further 3 to 5 minutes and stir well.
3. Decant into a bowl and in the same pan heat a little more avocado oil and fry the shallots and ginger for 3 to 4 minutes until softened. Add the garlic, lemongrass and coconut sugar and fry for another 2 minutes until fragrant.
4. Add the mince back into the pan on a medium heat with the lime juice and zest and half of the coriander, mint and basil leaves. Stir well and remove from the heat.
5. At this point taste the mince and adjust to your liking. If it needs more saltiness add a little more fish sauce, or for freshness add more lime juice.
6. Plate with baby spinach leaves, shredded carrot, radish, coriander, mint leaves and Thai sweet basil leaves. Serve with tamarind sauce and herb dressing.

TAMARIND SAUCE

7. Refer to Tamarind Sauce recipe using approximately ½ cup for this recipe.

HERB DRESSING

8. Refer to the herb dressing in the Grilled Mackerel and Herb Dressing recipe.

SHEPHERD'S PIE

EASY
PREP: 10 MINUTES
COOKING: 1 HOUR
SERVES 6
CASSEROLE DISH & SAUCEPAN

This is such a comforting dish and is perfect for a family meal. The best thing about this is you don't have to worry about making it look fancy as the peaks and ridges on the mash make it more delicious and appealing.

Hint: As a variation I have made this recipe using minced turkey but it can easily be substituted for the more traditional mince lamb.

INGREDIENTS

MINCE

1 TBSP olive oil

1kg turkey or lamb mince

1 TBSP onion powder

1 TBSP garlic powder

½ tsp salt

VEGETABLES

2 TBSP olive oil

1 medium onion chopped

4 garlic cloves finely chopped

1 leek finely chopped

1 cup mushrooms chopped

1 cup carrots chopped

1 TBSP fresh thyme

1 TBSP fresh rosemary

1 TBSP fresh parsley

1 cup bone broth

1 handful spinach

1 TBSP coconut aminos

Salt to taste

MASHED SWEET POTATOES

4 large orange sweet potatoes, peeled and cut into 2–3 cm chunks

2 TBSP light olive oil

1 onion finely chopped

2 garlic cloves finely chopped

Salt to taste

COOKING STEPS

1 Preheat your oven to 220°C (fan).

MINCE

2 Add 1 TBSP olive oil to the casserole dish and on a medium heat fry the mince for 7 to 10 minutes until cooked, stirring occasionally. Whilst cooking add the onion, garlic powders and salt. Decant into a bowl and drain and reserve any excess fat, (this applies more if using lamb mince).

VEGETABLES

3 In the same casserole dish add 2 TBSP olive oil. On a low to medium heat fry the onion and garlic for 3 to 4 minutes until softened, taking care not to brown the garlic.

4 Add the leeks, mushrooms, carrots and fresh herbs and fry on a low heat with the lid on for 8 to 10 minutes, stirring occasionally.

5 Next add the bone broth and simmer for 5 minutes before adding the spinach, coconut aminos and salt. Mix in the mince and remove from the heat.

MASHED SWEET POTATOES

6 Whilst the vegetables are cooking gently boil the sweet potatoes in salted water until soft (approximately 20 minutes). Once cooked, drain the potatoes and keep to one side.

7 In the same pan, heat the oil and lightly cook the onion and garlic for 2 to 3 minutes until soft but not too browned. Return the potatoes to the pan and mash with either a potato masher or, for a creamier texture, use a hand blender. Add salt to taste and mix well.

8 Top the mince with mashed sweet potatoes and bake in the oven for 20 minutes. Serve and enjoy.

MY AIP VERSION OF MY MUM'S BEEF STEW

EASY
PREP: 30 MINUTES
COOKING: 6 to 7 HOURS
SERVES 2 WITH PLENTY FOR LEFTOVERS
FRYING PAN OR WOK & SLOW COOKER

This was one of my favourite aromas to be greeted by when I returned home from school in the winter. Feeling cold from the walk home, stew for dinner was like walking into Paradise. We lovingly called this runny nose dinner when we were children! —*Claire*

Hint: Keep the beef cubes large to prevent the meat from drying out.

INGREDIENTS

500g beef stewing steak

1–2 TBSP cassava flour or arrowroot powder

Salt to taste

2 TBSP olive oil (you may require more oil if cooking in batches)

2 onions sliced

2 large carrots sliced into 2 cm chunks

1–2 parsnips sliced into 2 cm chunks (same volume as carrots)

½ swede chopped into 2 cm chunks (half volume as carrots)

2–3 cups bone broth

2 dried bay leaves

1 tsp dried thyme (or 3–4 sprigs of fresh)

1 tsp dried rosemary (or 3 sprigs of fresh)

2 TBSP coconut aminos

FOR THICKENING SAUCE:

1 TBSP arrowroot powder dissolved in 2 TBSP water (optional)

COOKING STEPS

1 Turn on the slow cooker to start heating.

2 In a large, sealable freezer bag add the cassava flour or arrowroot powder, salt and diced beef. Seal the bag and shake it until all the beef is coated.

3 In a large frying pan or skillet heat the olive oil. Add the beef in batches so there is space around each cube and sear each side for a minute or two. Repeat until all the beef is browned then place the seared beef into the slow cooker.

4 In the same frying pan add all of the chopped vegetables and sauté for about 5 minutes until the onions start to soften, (you may need a little more oil at this stage).

5 Add the broth, bay leaves, thyme, rosemary and coconut aminos and bring to the boil.

6 Transfer the contents to the slow cooker and stir. The liquid doesn't have to cover the other ingredients as the veggies will release their juices too.

7 Leave to cook for 6–7 hours. I like to make this in the morning on a weekend and then go out for the day, knowing I will be coming home to a delicious meal, already prepared—just like when I used to come home from school to this on dark, cold winter evenings.

8 When you are ready to eat, check the thickness of the sauce. If it needs thickening, dissolve a tablespoon of arrowroot powder in a little water, add to the slow cooker and stir. Let the arrowroot cook fully for about 5 minutes.

9 Meanwhile, steam some broccoli or cauliflower (perhaps some plain boiled potatoes for the family) and enjoy together.

MOROCCAN LAMB SHANKS WITH APRICOTS

EASY

PREP: 15 MINUTES
COOKING: 3 to 6 HOURS

SERVES 2

FRYING PAN, SLOW COOKER, CASSEROLE DISH OR TAGINE

The brilliant thing about lamb shanks in a slow cooker, is that it is almost impossible to overcook them.

Hint: In a slow cooker allow 5–6 hours, in a casserole dish or tagine in the oven 3 hours on low heat, 150°C. Cooking times stay the same for more lamb shanks . You know when it's cooked as it will be falling off the bone.

INGREDIENTS

BROWNING

1 TBSP of light olive oil

2 lamb shanks

COOKING

1 onion thinly sliced

2 tsp of dried coriander leaves

1 TBSP light olive oil

2 cinnamon sticks

500ml homemade bone broth

3 tsp of arrowroot powder mixed with 4 to 5 tsp cold water

Water for topping up bone broth if required

3 sprigs of fresh coriander

100g dried apricots (or substitute for prunes or pitted dates)

Salt to taste

2 TBSP of honey or maple syrup

1 lemon zested

Handful of coriander leaves chopped

COOKING STEPS

1 Preheat your oven to 150°C (fan) or turn on your slow cooker.

BROWNING

2 Heat the oil in frying pan and brown the lamb shanks on a high heat, turning occasionally, until a deep brown colour on all sides. Transfer the shanks to a plate and set aside.

COOKING THE LAMB

3 Soften onions in the frying pan adding an extra drop of oil if needed, then add dried coriander leaves and cinnamon sticks to the onions and stir.

4 Fry for 2 minutes until you can smell the cinnamon, before transferring to the slow cooker or casserole dish. Place the lamb shanks, with any juices, on top of the onions.

5 Dissolve the arrowroot powder in a little water and pour in with the bone broth. You are aiming for the lamb shanks to be half covered in the liquid, so you can add additional water if required. Add the fresh coriander, place the lid on and leave to cook.

6 Halfway through cooking check on the shanks, turning them and topping up with water or bone broth if less than a third to half of the shanks are covered.

7 At one hour before cooking time finishes, add the dried apricots (or tinned prunes or dates).

8 At half an hour before the end of the cooking time, add salt to taste, pour in the honey or maple syrup and sprinkle over the lemon zest, stirring the sauce carefully to combine.

9 At the end of the cooking time remove the coriander stalks and cinnamon sticks. Sprinkle over the coriander leaves and serve with roasted vegetables, cauliflower rice or couscous for the family.

LAMB MEATBALLS

EASY
PREP: 15 MINUTES
COOKING: 30 MINUTES
SERVES 3 to 4
BLENDER & GRATER

These meatballs are flavoured with mint and fenugreek leaves and are so flavoursome. They take a matter of minutes to prepare and can be cooking in the oven, doing their thing, giving you a little time back in your day for you.

INGREDIENTS

500g minced lamb

¼ tsp pink Himalayan salt

1 TBSP fish sauce or blended anchovies

1 TBSP garlic powder

1 large onion chopped

6 cloves garlic chopped

2 TBSP fresh ginger grated

2 TBSP dried fenugreek leaves

3 TBSP fresh mint chopped

½ tsp turmeric powder

COOKING STEPS

1. Preheat your oven to 225°C (fan) and line a tray with baking paper. Mix all of the ingredients together until they are thoroughly combined. (I blend a 50g tin of drained anchovies with 3 TBSP water and store in the fridge to use if I don't have any fish sauce).
2. Using your hands shape the mixture into 16 balls, approximately 4 cm in size, placing evenly on a baking tray.
3. Cook the meatballs in the oven at 225°C for 25 to 30 minutes, turning halfway, until the outside turns golden brown.

SAUSAGE ROLLS

EASY

PREP: 30 MINUTES
COOKING: 30 MINUTES

SERVES 4

FRYING PAN & GRATER

These sausage rolls are perfect enjoyed hot or cold with home-made pickles.

You can either make one large sausage roll or several small ones. Once sliced they can be shared with friends and family and are portable so can easily be eaten on the go as a tasty lunch or snack.

Hints: If making small sausage rolls reduce your heat to 200°C (fan) for the duration of the cooking time. The dough is best prepared with water that has just been boiled. If not rolling out straight away leave the dough covered to prevent it from drying out.

INGREDIENTS

SAUSAGE MEAT

400g pork mince

1 ½ TBSP fresh sage chopped

¼ tsp salt

1 small pinch of mace (optional)

1 tsp garlic powder

VEGETABLE FILLING

1 TBSP olive oil

1 ½ TBSP fresh sage

1 onion diced

3 cloves garlic chopped

1 carrot grated

1 small apple grated

1 leek finely sliced

Salt to taste

PASTRY

1 cup cassava flour (you may require more or less depending on your brand of flour)

⅛ tsp salt

1 tsp garlic powder

1 tsp onion powder

1 TBSP olive oil

Up to ¾ cup boiling water added gradually

COOKING STEPS

1 Preheat your oven to 220°C (fan).

SAUSAGE MEAT

2 In a large bowl add the pork mince, sage, salt, mace (optional) and garlic powder. Mix thoroughly to combine before setting aside.

VEGETABLE FILLING

3 Heat the olive oil in a frying pan and add the sage, onion and garlic. Add the carrots, apples and leeks to the pan and fry on a medium heat for 5 minutes until they are cooked. Season with salt, stir and transfer to a plate. Once cooled mix with the sausage meat and form a sausage-like shape before setting aside.

PASTRY

4 In a large bowl mix the cassava flour with the salt, onion and garlic powder before adding the olive oil and mixing.

5 Add boiling water gradually and mix thoroughly with a spatula. (You may need more or less boiling water depending on the brand of your cassava flour). You are looking for a consistency where the dough easily forms a ball and leaves the bowl clean when mixed with the spatula. Add more flour if the dough is too sticky or more water if too dry.

6 When the dough is cool enough to handle, knead it lightly for 1 minute until smooth and roll out to a rectangle shape between two sheets of baking paper to a 5mm thickness.

7 Firmly press the sausage meat into a sausage-like shape and place onto the middle of the rolled out dough and use the baking paper to roll the pastry firmly around the meat. Secure the ends of the pastry and coat the pastry in olive oil.

8 If making one large sausage roll cook for 25 to 30 minutes, (15 minutes at 220°C, then to turn the pastry golden and crispy cook for a further 10 to 15 minutes at 230°C).

LAMB & SWEDE PASTIES

MEDIUM

PREP: 30 MINUTES
COOKING: 30 MINUTES

SERVES 10

FRYING PAN

INGREDIENTS

SWEDE

1 ½ cups swede diced into 2cm cubes

½ TBSP olive oil

1 TBSP fresh thyme

½ TBSP garlic powder

¼ tsp salt

FILLING

400g lamb mince

1 TBSP garlic powder

½ TBSP onion powder

1 cup carrots diced into 2 cm cubes

1 onion diced

1 TBSP ginger peeled & chopped

4 garlic cloves finely chopped

1 tsp thyme

1 tsp fresh rosemary

1 ½ cups white sweet potato diced into 2 cm cubes

Salt to taste

½ TBSP garlic powder

PASTRY (MAKES 10)

3 cups cassava flour

¼ tsp salt

3 tsp garlic powder

3 tsp onion powder

3 TBSP olive oil

Up to 2 cups boiling water added gradually

3 to 4 TBSP olive oil for greasing tray and pasties

These delicious lamb and swede pasties are perfect enjoyed hot or cold with a simple salad. They are perfectly portable and can easily be eaten as a tasty lunch on a busy day or warmed in the oven the next day if they last that long!

Hint: The dough is best prepared with water that has just been boiled. If not rolling out straight away leave the dough covered to prevent it from drying out.

You can easily interchange the fillings and swap the swede for curry sweet potato—just delicious!

COOKING STEPS

SWEDE

1 Preheat your oven to 180°C (fan). Peel and cube the swede and mix in a bowl with olive oil, thyme, garlic powder and salt. Transfer to a lined baking tray and leave to roast in the centre of the oven for 40 minutes or until cooked and golden in colour.

FILLING

2 Heat your frying pan to a medium heat, add the lamb mince and fry with the garlic and onion powder for 5 minutes until cooked and slightly browned. Decant the lamb to cool, draining and reserving the oil separately.

3 In the same frying pan, on a medium heat add the diced carrots and onions, stirring well. If more oil is required for cooking at this stage add a little of the lamb fat 1 TBSP at a time to the pan. After 5 minutes add the ginger and fry for a further 5 minutes, stirring intermittently. Lower the heat slightly and add the garlic, thyme, rosemary and diced white sweet potatoes, adding more lamb fat if required. Season with salt to taste and ½ TBSP garlic powder and cook for 10 minutes, stirring occasionally.

4 Add the cooked lamb back into the pan and mix with the vegetables, then transfer to a large plate or bowl to cool. When the swede has roasted leave to cool and then mix with the lamb filling mixture. Turn the oven temperature up to 200°C in preparation for cooking your pasties.

PASTRY

5 In a large bowl mix the cassava flour with the salt, onion and garlic powders before adding the olive oil and mixing. Bear in mind that you may require slightly more or less flour depending on your brand of flour.

6 Add boiling water gradually and mix thoroughly with a spatula. (You may need more or less boiling water depending on the brand of your cassava flour). You are looking for a consistency where the dough easily forms a ball and leaves the bowl clean when mixed with the spatula. Add more flour if the dough is too sticky or more boiling water if too dry.

7 When the dough is cool enough to handle, knead it lightly for 1 minute until smooth. Split the dough evenly into 10 equal balls and leave covered.

8 Taking one ball of dough at a time roll out to a circle shape between 2 sheets of baking paper to a 4 to 5mm thickness. Place the filling onto the one side of the rolled out dough in a semi-circle shape, spreading as evenly as possible. Take care to leave around a 2 cm gap at the edge of the circle to seal your pasty. Lift the other side of the dough carefully over the filling and seal the edges, carefully pressing down with your thumb. You can crimp the edges of the pasty using your index finger and thumb to fold the edges of the pastry turning the edges of the dough over on itself, going from one edge to the other. Alternatively you can use the edges of the fork to seal the edges of the pastry.

9 Line your baking tray with baking paper and using your fingertips evenly coat with 1 TBSP olive oil. As each pasty is sealed, carefully lift and transfer to this tray and gently coat with a little olive oil using your fingertips. (As the pastry is delicate I find it is useful to have an egg cup handy filled with olive oil, so that I can dip my fingers in at this stage). Continue to roll out, fill and seal your pasties and lay them out on your oven tray, (you may require two trays). Once all of your pasties are formed and ready to bake, cook for 30 minutes at 200°C until the pastry is golden and crispy.

LAMB & BUTTERNUT SQUASH CURRY

MEDIUM

PREP: 20 MINUTES
COOKING: 1 HOUR 20 MINUTES

SERVES 6

OVEN PROOF CASSEROLE DISH
BLENDER

This lamb curry is beautifully tasty and is guaranteed to bring a smile to your face. It is both hearty and warming and can be enjoyed with roti or cauliflower rice.

Hint: To maximise leftovers, before reheating add 1 tsp of a chopped preserved lemon, ¼ tsp mace and a small handful of olives and chopped dried apricots to create a delicious tagine-inspired dish.

INGREDIENTS

2 TBSP olive, coconut or avocado oil

2 onions sliced

6 cloves chopped garlic

1 TBSP ginger

6 sprigs thyme

2 bay leaves

1 small handful of curry leaves

900g lamb diced

½ tsp salt

1 TBSP garlic powder

1 tsp cinnamon powder

1 tsp turmeric powder

½ tsp cloves ground

100g cooked beetroot blended

150g pineapple blended

200ml chicken bone broth

200ml coconut milk

250g butternut squash cubed

1 lime juiced

1 handful of fresh coriander chopped

FOR THICKENING SAUCE

2 tsp tapioca starch mixed with
2 tsp water

TAGINE

1 tsp of a chopped preserved lemon, ¼ tsp mace, olives and a small handful of chopped dried apricots

COOKING STEPS

1 Preheat your oven to 200°C (fan).

2 In your casserole dish heat the oil and fry the sliced onions on a medium heat until softened and light brown in colour. Add the chopped garlic, ginger, thyme, bay and curry leaves and sauté for a further 4 to 5 minutes on a low heat.

3 Keeping the heat low add the diced lamb (approx. 2 cm sized chunks), salt and garlic powder, cinnamon, turmeric and ground cloves, stirring well to combine.

4 Whilst the lamb is gently cooking prepare the sauce by blending the beetroot and pineapple together. Add to the lamb and stir well.

5 Turn the heat up slightly and add in the bone broth, coconut milk and butternut squash (approx. 2 cm sized chunks) and stir to combine.

6 Place the lid on the casserole dish and cook for 1 hour in the middle of the oven at 200°C.

7 After 1 hour the lamb should be tender. Remove the casserole dish from the oven and transfer to the hob on a low heat with the lid off. If the sauce requires thickening add the tapioca starch mixture and stir well. The sauce should thicken after 2 to 3 minutes. Stir in the lime juice and coriander and serve with roti or cauliflower rice.

SIDES & FAMILY FAVOURITES

HOMEMADE GNOCCHI & PESTO

MEDIUM

PREP: 20 MINUTES
COOKING: 20 MINUTES

SERVES 6

BLENDER & POTATO MASHER

There's nothing better than homemade pesto and gnocchi and this pesto recipe, made with anchovies and capers, is packed full of nutrients and flavour. It is perfect with gnocchi, chicken, fish or courgette spaghetti, or simply used as a pizza topping. The gnocchi can also be used as dumplings in casseroles.

Pesto hint: Keep the pesto in a sterilised jar in the fridge for up to a week or freeze in ice cube trays and defrost and use as you need to.

Gnocchi hint: The gnocchi can be easily frozen after step 4 and used as required, boiling for approximately 5 minutes or until the gnocchi rises to the surface of the water.

INGREDIENTS

PESTO

1 lemon (juice and rind)

60g rocket leaves

60g fresh basil

30g fresh sage

8 anchovy fillets

1 TBSP nutritional yeast

2 TBSP rinsed, drained capers

2 garlic cloves

80 ml extra-virgin olive oil

2 tsp maple syrup

GNOCCHI

1 large white sweet potato diced (3 ½ cups)

¼ tsp salt

1 tsp of garlic powder

½ cup cassava flower (you may require slightly more or less depending on your brand of flour)

COOKING STEPS

PESTO

1. Zest and juice the lemon and set aside. Add the rocket, basil, sage, anchovies, nutritional yeast, capers, garlic and olive oil to your blender with the zest and juice of the lemon and maple syrup. Blend until smooth.
2. Taste and adjust the consistency by adding a little water to loosen if required and blend to combine.

GNOCCHI

3. Peel, dice and boil the white sweet potato for 10 to 12 minutes until cooked. Drain and mash into a smooth consistency. Add salt and garlic powder and combine well.
4. Gradually add the cassava flour until the mixture forms a dough-like ball. Once the mixture is cool enough to handle coat your hands in a little olive oil to prevent the mixture from sticking to them. Using your hands form small oval shapes and press down on each one lightly with the back of a fork to flatten slightly. Place on a plate sprinkled with cassava flour to prevent the gnocchi from sticking.
5. Drop in boiling water for 3 to 5 minutes or until the gnocchi rises to the surface of the water and drain immediately.
6. Plate by drizzling with your scrumptious pesto and some lightly fried mushrooms and anchovy fillets.
7. For a crispier texture and instead of boiling, the gnocchi can be pan fried for 2 to 4 minutes after stage 4.

POTATO & LEEK CAKES

MEDIUM

PREP: 20 MINUTES
COOKING: 20 MINUTES

SERVES 8

POTATO MASHER

These potato cakes remind me of the taste of bubble and squeak. The white sweet potatoes provide the perfect amount of sweetness and the onion and leek add an incredible caramelised flavour. A perfect healthy carbohydrate accompaniment to any AIP meal. They are so versatile that you really can incorporate anything you fancy such as bacon and cabbage or carrots and spinach. It is a great way to use leftover vegetables as the mash can be tweaked to incorporate swede or parsnips too. I like to serve these with pan fried salmon and kale or for breakfast with crispy bacon, mushrooms, spinach and avocado.

—Sue

Hint: If you enjoy batch cooking you can store these between small pieces of baking paper, pop them in the freezer and reheat in your oven to enjoy on another day.

INGREDIENTS

1 large white sweet potato diced (3 ½ cups)

½ tsp salt

2 TBSP olive oil

1 onion finely sliced

1 leek finely chopped

4 garlic cloves finely chopped

½ cup cassava flour

2 TBSP olive oil (for greasing baking tray)

1 TBSP olive oil (for coating hands)

COOKING STEPS

1. Preheat your oven to 220°C (fan).
2. Peel, dice and boil the white sweet potato for 10 to 12 minutes until cooked. Drain and mash into a smooth consistency. Add salt and combine well.
3. Finely slice the onion and leek and fry gently in olive oil for 4 to 5 minutes until slightly caramelised. Add the garlic and cook for another 2 to 3 minutes on a low heat. Transfer the cooked onion, leek and garlic into the same bowl as the mash and combine well.
4. Gradually add the cassava flour until the mixture forms a dough-like ball and grease your baking tray with 2 tablespoons of olive oil.
5. Once the mixture is cool enough to handle coat your hands in a little olive oil to prevent the mixture from sticking to them. Using your hands form the mash into eight small round balls. Flatten each ball with the palm of your hands forming a burger-like shape.
6. Place the potato cakes onto your baking tray and turn each one over, using your fingers to coat each one in oil. Place in an oven at 220°C and cook for 15 to 20 minutes, turning the cakes over halfway through the cooking time.

COURGETTE SPAGHETTI WITH BASIL

EASY

PREP: 10 MINUTES
COOKING: 10 MINUTES

SERVES 2

JULIENNE PEELER OR MANDOLINE, WOK OR LARGE FRYING PAN

These courgettes provide a surprisingly satisfying alternative to pasta, making this dish fresh, vibrant and healthy.

Hint: Dry your shredded courgettes as much as you can to prevent them from releasing water when cooking.

INGREDIENTS

4 courgettes finely shredded

1 TBSP olive oil

3 garlic cloves chopped

Handful of fresh basil leaves finely chopped

Salt to taste

COOKING STEPS

1. Finely shred the outer sides of the courgettes lengthways using a julienne peeler. Once you reach the inner core of your courgettes, if they are quite soft then do not continue to shred these. Instead save them for another recipe, as they may release a little too much water when cooked for this dish. Dry any excess liquid from the shredded courgettes with kitchen paper.
2. Add the olive oil to the pan and on a low to medium heat fry the garlic for 2 to 3 minutes until fragrant.
3. Turn the heat up to high and fry the shredded courgettes and chopped basil for approximately 3 to 4 minutes until slightly softened.
4. Add salt to taste and mix well. Remove from the heat and serve.

MASHED SWEET POTATOES

EASY

PREP: 10 MINUTES
COOKING: 20 MINUTES

SERVES 2

POTATO MASHER OR HAND BLENDER

These sweet potatoes are wonderfully tasty and can literally be eaten with any fish, meat or casserole.

Hint: This pairs well with duck in orange sauce, lamb chops or salmon and cabbage.

INGREDIENTS

2 large orange sweet potatoes, peeled and cut into 2 to 3 cm chunks

2 to 3 TBSP light olive oil

2 TBSP onion finely chopped

1 garlic clove finely chopped

Salt to taste

COOKING STEPS

1. Gently boil the sweet potatoes in salted water until soft (approximately 12 to 16 minutes). Once cooked, drain the potatoes and keep to one side.
2. In the same pan, heat the oil and lightly cook the onion and garlic for 2 to 3 minutes until soft, taking care not to caramelise them.
3. Remove from the heat and return the potatoes to the pan and mash with either a potato masher or, for a creamier texture, use a hand blender. Add a little extra salt to taste if you wish and enjoy.

CITRUS-DRESSED CASSAVA

EASY

PREP: 10 MINUTES
COOKING: 15 to 25 MINUTES

SERVES 1

PEELER, GRATER,
SAUCEPAN & BLENDER

This is such a fresh, zingy dish that will tantalise your tastebuds and provide a perfect snack or an accompaniment to fish, seafood or chicken.

INGREDIENTS

⅓ cassava peeled and cut into thick chips (enough for 1 serving)

¼ tsp salt

DRESSING

1 to 2 garlic cloves roughly chopped (depending on your personal taste)

1 lime juiced & zested

1 small orange juiced

3 TBSP olive oil

1 TBSP chopped parsley

COOKING STEPS

1. Peel and cut cassava into thick chips, taking care to remove the hard fibrous core. Wash thoroughly two or three times.
2. Boil the chips for 15 to 25 minutes (depending on the thickness of your chips), or until the cassava has softened and is cooked. (If you are able to pierce the chip easily with a small knife it is cooked). Drain and transfer to a large bowl.
3. Place all of the dressing ingredients apart from the parsley into a blender and blitz into a smooth dressing. Add the parsley and stir.
4. At this point the cassava chips may be cool enough to handle as you may want to cut them into cubes before adding your dressing (optional).
5. Drizzle the desired amount of dressing over the cooked cassava and mix carefully, taking care not to break the cassava. The cassava should soak up some of the incredibly flavoured dressing. Taste and season with more salt if required.
6. You may have some dressing leftover which can be stored in a clean jar in the fridge for another day.

ROTI

EASY

PREP: 10 MINUTES
COOKING: 20 MINUTES

SERVES 8

LARGE SHALLOW FRYING PAN
OR PANCAKE PAN

I would not have survived the AIP journey if it wasn't for the occasional roti or 'flat bread'. I longed for a bread-like substitute and was over the moon with the results of these rotis. They are extremely quick to prepare, soft and supple and can be easily reheated the next day or eaten cold as a wrap. These usually keep in the fridge for 3 to 4 days and can be reheated in a pan to soften.

Because they are so versatile you can add as much flavour as you like, depending on what you are planning on eating them with. —*Sue*

A few wrap ideas:

- Lamb meatballs, rainbow salad and coconut yogurt
- Smoked salmon, watercress, shredded carrot and avocado
- Shredded chicken, guacamole, rocket and spinach
- Tuna mixed with spring onion, coconut yogurt and garlic powder, radish and lettuce

INGREDIENTS

2 cups cassava flour (you may require slightly more or less depending on your brand of flour)

⅛ tsp salt

1 TBSP garlic powder

½ TBSP onion powder

2 TBSP olive oil

Up to 2 cups boiling water added gradually

ADDITIONAL EXTRAS

¼ tsp turmeric powder

¼ tsp curry leaf powder

1 TSBP dried fenugreek leaves (chopped)

COOKING STEPS

1. In a large bowl mix the cassava flour with the salt, onion and garlic powders before adding the olive oil and mixing.
2. Add boiling water gradually and mix thoroughly with a spatula. (You may need more or less boiling water depending on the brand of your cassava flour). You are looking for a consistency where the dough easily forms a ball and leaves the bowl clean when mixed with the spatula. Add more flour if the dough is too sticky or more water if too dry.
3. Divide the dough into small balls depending on the size you would like your rotis, also bearing in mind the size of your pan. Cover the bowl with a tea towel to prevent the dough from drying out.
4. Roll out each ball of dough between two sheets of baking paper into a circular shape, aiming for an even thickness of approximately 2 to 3 mm.
5. Heat the pan and cook on a medium to high heat for 1 to 2 minutes until little air bubbles appear on the surface. Once this happens turn the roti over and lightly press on the edges, or any uncooked areas with a spatula. Using the spatula or your hand, gently turn the roti in circular motions on both sides until cooked and if you are lucky it will inflate.
6. Place the cooked roti on a metal cooling rack or a sheet of baking paper to cool slightly. I like to store mine in an airtight container, with small layers of baking paper between each roti to prevent them from sticking.

CAULIFLOWER RICE

EASY

PREP: 10 MINUTES
COOKING: 10 MINUTES

SERVES 4 to 6

BLENDER OR GRATER & FRYING PAN OR WOK

I used to live on rice so this cauliflower rice recipe makes a great alternative. It only takes 10 minutes to cook and it goes well with so many dishes. I like to eat it with pak choi and grilled fish or honey glazed chicken. It stores well in the fridge so you can make this in advance and warm it as needed.

—Sue

Hint: As another recipe alternative you may like to add some chopped carrots, leeks and mushrooms with 1 ½ TBSP fish sauce and 2 TBSP coconut aminos to create an Asian-inspired cauliflower fried rice.

Alternatively, for an Indian-inspired cauliflower rice add ½ TBSP turmeric, 1 TBSP dried fenugreek leaves, 1 TBSP curry leaves and a handful of finely chopped cavolo nero.

INGREDIENTS

2 TBSP olive or avocado oil

1 onion finely chopped

1 TBSP ginger chopped

3 large cloves garlic chopped

1 large cauliflower blended or grated

1 ½ TBSP garlic powder

4 spring onion finely chopped

Salt to taste

2 TBSP fresh coriander chopped

COOKING STEPS

1. Heat the oil in a wok, add the onion and ginger and fry for 2 to 3 minutes on a medium to high heat until lightly golden in colour. Reduce the heat and add in the chopped garlic and stir well.
2. Blend the cauliflower to a rice-like consistency in small batches using a food processor, blender or grater.
3. Add the cauliflower rice, garlic powder and spring onion to the pan and stir well. Fry for 7 to 8 minutes until the cauliflower rice is tender.
4. Season with salt, remove from heat and stir in the chopped coriander before serving.

SWEET POTATO CURRY

EASY

PREP: 10 MINUTES
COOKING: 35 to 40 MINUTES

SERVES 4

LARGE FRYING PAN OR WOK

This sweet potato curry is made with fragrant turmeric, garlic, ginger and curry leaves and makes such a flavoursome side dish.

Hint: This is best served with roti or cauliflower rice and tamarind sauce.

INGREDIENTS

3 TBSP olive or avocado oil

1 medium onion finely chopped

2 TBSP ginger finely chopped

6 garlic cloves finely chopped

1 tsp curry leaf powder

2 ½ tsp turmeric powder

15 curry leaves

3 TBSP dried fenugreek leaves

1 medium white sweet potato diced in 2 cm cubes (2 ½ cups)

2 TBSP tamarind sauce (refer to Tamarind Sauce recipe

1 TBSP fish sauce

½ TBSP garlic powder

½ tsp salt

1 drop food grade black pepper essential oil (optional)

1 TBSP fresh coriander chopped

COOKING STEPS

1 Heat the oil in a large pan and cook the onion and ginger on a low to medium heat for 7 to 10 minutes until soft and caramelised. Add the garlic, curry leaf powder, turmeric, curry and fenugreek leaves and cook for 2 to 4 minutes until fragrant, stirring occasionally.

2 Add in the diced white sweet potato and stir well. Leave to cook on a low to medium heat with the lid on for 10 to 15 minutes, stirring occasionally, ensuring the potatoes do not stick to the pan. If they are sticking add a little water if required. After 10 minutes test to see if the potato is cooked. If not cook for a further 4 to 5 minutes. At this point the potatoes should have turned a beautiful shade of yellow.

3 Remove the lid and add the tamarind sauce, fish sauce, garlic powder and salt. Stir well and cook on a higher heat for 3 to 4 minutes to achieve a crispier texture on the outside of the potatoes. If you would like to add in food grade black pepper essential oil for a slightly spicy flavour add it in now and stir to combine.

4 Garnish with fresh coriander and serve with cauliflower rice or roti.

SPINACH CURRY

EASY
PREP: 10 MINUTES
COOKING: 15 MINUTES
SERVES 4
LARGE FRYING PAN OR WOK

This nutritious spinach curry is made with fragrant fenugreek and curry leaves and makes such a flavoursome quick and easy side dish.

Hint: This is best served with roti or cauliflower rice and tamarind sauce.

INGREDIENTS

3 TBSP olive or avocado oil

1 medium onion finely chopped

2 TBSP ginger finely chopped

6 garlic cloves finely chopped

1 tsp curry leaf powder

1 tsp turmeric powder

15 curry leaves

2 TBSP dried fenugreek leaves

250g baby spinach

2 TBSP tamarind sauce, (refer to Tamarind Sauce recipe

½ TBSP garlic powder

½ tsp salt

1 drop food grade black pepper essential oil (optional)

1 TBSP fresh coriander chopped

COOKING STEPS

1. Heat the oil in a large pan and cook the onion and ginger on a low to medium heat for 7 to 10 minutes until soft and caramelised. Add the garlic, curry leaf powder, turmeric, curry and fenugreek leaves and cook for 2 to 4 minutes until fragrant, stirring occasionally.
2. Add in the spinach and stir well. Leave to cook on a low to medium heat with the lid on for 3 to 4 minutes, stirring occasionally until wilted.
3. Remove the lid and add the tamarind sauce, garlic powder and salt. Stir well and cook on a higher heat for 2 to 3 minutes. If you would like to add in food grade black pepper essential oil for a slightly spicy flavour add it in now and stir to combine.
4. Garnish with fresh coriander and serve with cauliflower rice or roti.

CLAIRE'S GUACAMOLE

EASY

PREP: 10 MINUTES

SERVES 4

FORK & BOWL

When I lived in Tucson, Arizona I fell in love with guacamole and it was a staple part of our diet... always homemade because it's so quick and easy and great for when all your avos ripen at the same time. As a toddler my son lived off this! —*Claire*

Hint: I learned about adding lime essential oil accidently once when I couldn't find limes—I used a lemon plus lime essential oil instead and it worked brilliantly.

INGREDIENTS

2 ripe avocados

1 lime, zest and juice

1 clove garlic

1 TBSP finely chopped red onion

1 drop food grade lime essential oil (optional)

Salt to taste

STEPS

1. Peel and pit the avocados and mash with a fork—I like to keep it quite lumpy.
2. Crush the garlic clove into the mix, the juice of 1 lime and the chopped onion and mix with a fork. Add salt to taste.
3. For an extra refreshing zing on a hot day add some lime zest or one drop of food grade lime essential oil. This will also delay the guacamole from going brown. Eat immediately or keep in an airtight container in the fridge for 48 hours.

VEGETABLE MANCHURIAN STIR FRY

MEDIUM
PREP: 10 MINUTES
COOKING: 15 MINUTES
SERVES 2
FOOD PROCESSOR OR GRATER, DEEP SAUCEPAN & FRYING PAN OR WOK

We love flavour in our house and when my husband made a non-AIP version of this vegetable manchurian stir fry, it didn't take long for me to create an AIP version.

Although the recipe involves deep frying, the vegetable balls are really light and are not at all greasy. This dish satisfies your crunchy, flavour-filled, sweet and sour cravings and can be eaten on its own or as a tasty accompaniment to grilled fish. It is great for using up your leftover vegetables and the cabbage can easily be substituted for Chinese cabbage or kale. —*Sue*

Hint: These are perfect for making in advance and freezing. The vegetable balls can easily be reheated in the oven and stirred into the sauce before serving.

INGREDIENTS

VEGETABLE BALLS

2 cups cabbage grated

1 tsp curry leaves

½ tsp turmeric powder

¼ tsp cinnamon powder

1 tsp dried fenugreek leaves

3–4 TBSP cassava flour (you may require slightly more or less depending on your brand of flour)

1 tsp ginger chopped or grated

1 tsp garlic chopped

½ tsp salt

Enough light olive oil to deep fry the vegetable balls

STIR FRY

2 TBSP olive oil

1 small onion chopped

2 tsp ginger chopped or grated

1 TBSP garlic chopped

1 large carrot shredded

½ leek finely chopped

1 TBSP coconut aminos

1 TBSP Homemade Ketchup (Refer to the Homemade Ketchup recipe)

1–2 tsp tapioca starch mixed with ½ cup water

1 handful of fresh coriander chopped

2 spring onions finely sliced

COOKING STEPS

VEGETABLE BALLS

1. Grate the cabbage by hand or using a food processor and transfer to a large mixing bowl. Add the curry leaves, turmeric, cinnamon, dried chopped fenugreek leaves, cassava flour, chopped ginger, garlic and salt. Mix thoroughly and set aside.
2. In a deep saucepan heat the light olive oil to 325 to 350°F. Using your hands shape the cabbage mixture into balls approximately 3 to 4 cm in size. Deep fry the vegetable balls for 4 to 5 minutes, Take care not to overload the pan. Halfway through cooking turn the veg balls over. Cook until a crispy golden coating has formed and the balls float to the surface of the oil. You may need to fry in batches depending on the size of your saucepan.
3. Carefully remove the vegetable balls from the oil and place onto kitchen paper to drain.

STIR FRY

4. Heat 2 TBSP olive oil in a large non-stick frying pan on a medium-high heat. Fry the onion and ginger for 3 to 4 minutes until lightly browned. Stir in the garlic and fry for 1 minute before adding in the shredded carrots and leeks.
5. Taking care not to overcook the vegetables add in the coconut aminos and Homemade Ketchup and stir well. In a small cup or bowl mix the tapioca starch with the water and add to the pan. Cook for another 1 to 2 minutes to cook tapioca starch. You should end up with a thick sauce similar to the consistency of jam.
6. Carefully stir in the vegetable balls, fresh coriander and spring onions and serve immediately.

CHICKEN NACHOS

MEDIUM

PREP: 20 MINUTES
COOKING: 40 MINUTES

SERVES 4

ROLLING PIN, FRYING PAN OR PANCAKE PAN & SMALL SAUCEPAN

This is a real treat, fun to eat and well worth the effort. They can also be used as crackers for pâté or eaten with sliced meats and salad for a lunch on the go.

INGREDIENTS

NACHOS

2 ½ cup cassava flour (you may require slightly more or less depending on your brand of flour)

1 tsp salt

1 tsp of turmeric powder

2 tsp of onion powder

2 tsp of garlic powder

½ cup of olive oil

Up to 1 cup of coconut milk (added gradually)

SALSA

½ TBSP olive oil

¼ onion finely diced

1 TBSP capers finely chopped

½ cup of Homemade Ketchup (refer to Homemade Ketchup recipe)

GUACAMOLE

Refer to Sue's Guacamole recipe for ingredients

CHEESE SAUCE

Refer to Cheese Sauce recipe for ingredients

CHICKEN

1 raw large chicken breast

Salt to taste

COOKING STEPS

NACHOS

1. In a large bowl mix the cassava flour with the salt, turmeric, onion and garlic powders before adding the olive oil and mixing.
2. Next gradually add the coconut milk and mix thoroughly with a spatula. (You may need more or less coconut milk depending on the consistency). You are looking for a consistency where the dough easily forms a ball and leaves the bowl clean when mixed with the spatula. Add more flour if the dough is too sticky or a little cold water if too dry.
3. Divide the dough into small balls depending on the size you would like nachos, also bearing in mind the size of your pan. Cover the bowl with a tea towel to prevent the dough from drying out.
4. Roll out each ball of dough between 2 sheets of baking paper into a circular shape, aiming for an even thickness of approximately 1 to 2 mm, or as thin as possible.
5. Heat the pan and cook on a low to medium heat for 3 to 4 minutes until little air bubbles appear on the surface. Once this happens turn it over and lightly press on the edges, or any uncooked areas with a spatula. Using the spatula or your hand, gently turn in circular motions on both sides until cooked and slightly crispy.
6. Once cooked place on a metal cooling rack or a sheet or baking paper to cool slightly and achieve a crispy texture, then cut into triangles using a sharp knife.

SALSA

7. Refer to the Homemade Ketchup recipe. In a small pan heat the olive oil and fry the diced onion for 2 to 3 minutes until softened. Add the capers and Homemade Ketchup. Stir and simmer for 2 to 3 minutes before decanting and cooling.

GUACAMOLE

8. Refer to Sue's Guacamole for recipe.

CHEESE SAUCE

9. Refer to the Cheese Sauce recipe.

CHICKEN

10. Season with salt and bake the chicken breasts for 20 to 25 minutes until cooked through. Once cooled enough to handle shred the chicken breasts, assemble altogether and serve.

SUE'S GUACAMOLE

EASY

PREP: 10 MINUTES

SERVES 4

FORK OR POTATO MASHER & GRATER

Due to our absolute love of guacamole we had to include two recipes to enjoy!

I love guacamole but my children love it even more. Avocados don't last long in our house and if there is a batch of guacamole that doesn't get eaten the same day, (which is very rare), it is always devoured the next morning with baby spinach, smoked salmon, mackerel or bacon and any leftover root veg. —*Sue*

Hint: If not serving straight away squeeze a few additional drops of lime over the guacamole to keep it from discolouring.

INGREDIENTS

2 large ripe avocados

1 clove garlic finely chopped or grated

2 TBSP finely chopped spring onion

1 large lime – juice and zest

2 TBSP finely chopped coriander leaves

Pink Himalayan salt to taste

1 tsp garlic powder

COOKING STEPS

1. Cut the avocados in half and carefully remove stone. Scoop out the flesh with a spoon, mash roughly with a fork or potato masher and set aside.
2. Peel the garlic clove, crush, finely chop or grate. Add to the mashed avocados with the chopped spring onion, half of the lime juice and all of the zest.
3. Stir in the coriander and add salt to taste. Mix and taste and if desired add more lime juice and garlic powder. Cover and chill until ready to serve.

SALT & APPLE CIDER VINEGAR CRISPS

EASY

PREP: 10 MINUTES
COOKING: 15 MINUTES

SERVES 2

SMALL DEEP SAUCEPAN FOR FRYING, MANDOLINE SLICER OR FOOD PROCESSOR

These crisps are a real treat and so quick to prepare, especially if you have a food processor that can slice the potatoes in a matter of minutes!

Hint: This works well with any root vegetable, including cassava root.

INGREDIENTS

Enough light olive oil to deep fry the crisps

2 white sweet potatoes finely sliced on a mandoline slicer or food processor

Salt to taste

Up to 2 TBSP organic apple cider vinegar filled in a small container with spray nozzle

COOKING STEPS

1 Heat the olive oil in saucepan to 325 to 350°F.

2 Using your mandoline slicer or food processor finely slice the white sweet potatoes.

3 Fry in small batches for 3 to 4 minutes, turning halfway, until the outside turns a light golden brown and the crisps float to the top of the surface of the oil.

4 Drain on kitchen paper to remove excess oil. Sprinkle with salt and spray lightly with apple cider vinegar and enjoy.

PAD THAI

EASY
PREP: 15 MINUTES
COOKING: 25 MINUTES
SERVES 2
JULIENNE PEELER OR MANDOLINE, WOK & SMALL SAUCEPAN

This dish has the fresh and vibrant flavours of Pad Thai but uses shredded carrot and courgettes to replace the noodles. It tastes incredible with some freshly squeezed lime and the fried shallots provide a little crunch. You can easily share with the family and replace the shredded carrot and courgettes with flat rice noodles and top with chopped peanuts.

Hint: Dry your shredded courgettes as much as you can to prevent them from releasing water when cooking.

INGREDIENTS

SAUCE

½ cup of Tamarind Sauce (refer to Tamarind Sauce recipe)

Add the following:

2 TBSP coconut sugar

2 TBSP fish sauce

CRISPY SHALLOTS

1 cup coconut oil

4 small shallots sliced

STIR FRY

3 TBSP coconut oil

1 onion sliced

3 garlic cloves finely chopped

2 chicken thighs diced

175g large raw peeled prawns

VEGETABLE NOODLES

2 large carrots peeled and finely shredded

3 courgettes finely shredded

1 TBSP coconut oil

TOPPINGS

1 lime freshly squeezed

6 Thai basil leaves roughly chopped

6 mint leaves roughly chopped

1 small handful of fresh coriander roughly chopped

6 radishes quartered

3 spring onions finely sliced

COOKING STEPS

SAUCE

1 Refer to the Tamarind Sauce recipe for method. Using ½ cup of the tamarind sauce add fish sauce and coconut aminos in a small saucepan. Heat gently and stir well for 3 to 4 minutes until fully combined.

CRISPY SHALLOTS

2 Slice the shallots and fry in coconut oil for 2 to 3 mins until golden and crispy. Drain on kitchen paper to remove excess oil.

STIR FRY & VEGETABLE NOODLES

3 Heat 2 TBSP oil in a large non-stick frying pan or wok and fry the sliced onions on a medium heat for 2 to 3 minutes until slightly softened. Add in the garlic and cook for another 2 minutes stirring continuously. Add in the remaining oil and diced chicken and cook for 5 to 7 minutes until gently browned. Next add the prawns to the pan with the chicken and cook for a few minutes until the prawns turn pink. Once the chicken is fully cooked stir through 2 to 3 TBSP of the tamarind-based sauce and decant the contents of the pan into a large bowl.

4 Peel the carrots and finely shred the outer sides of the courgettes lengthways using a julienne peeler. Once you reach the inner core of your courgettes, if they are quite soft then do not continue to shred these. Instead save them for another recipe, as they may release a little too much water when cooked for this dish. Dry any excess liquid from the shredded courgettes with kitchen paper. Add in 2 to 3 TBSP of the tamarind-based sauce to coat the vegetable noodles and stir well. Remove from the heat and mix with the chicken & prawns.

TOPPINGS

5 Sprinkle over the freshly squeezed lime, chopped Thai basil, mint, coriander, radishes and sliced spring onions. Finally, top with the crispy fried shallots and enjoy.

PIZZA

EASY

PREP: 15 MINUTES
COOKING: 25 MINUTES

SERVES 2

OVEN

This pizza really hits the spot, especially if the rest of the family are ordering in. You will feel like you are having such a treat but have the comfort of knowing that all of it is AIP. —*Sue*

INGREDIENTS

PIZZA BASE

1 cup cassava flour (you may require slightly more or less depending on your brand of flour)

1 TBSP oil

⅛ tsp salt

1 tsp garlic powder

Up to ¾ cup boiling water added gradually

PIZZA SAUCE

2 TBSP Homemade Ketchup (refer to Homemade Ketchup recipe)

Add the following:

½ tsp dried oregano

1 tsp onion powder

TOPPINGS

1 small onion sliced

2 mushrooms sliced

6 Greek kalamata olives pitted and halved

2 slices prosciutto torn into small pieces

¼ cup AIP cheese (refer to Cheese recipe for ingredients)

1 pinch of fresh basil leaves

1 tsp garlic powder

1 tsp olive oil

COOKING STEPS

1 Preheat your oven to 220°C (fan).

PIZZA BASE

2 In a large bowl combine the cassava flour with olive oil, salt and garlic powder.

3 Add boiling water gradually and mix thoroughly with a spatula. (You may need more or less boiling water depending on the brand of your cassava flour). You are looking for a consistency where the dough easily forms a ball and leaves the bowl clean when mixed with the spatula. Add more flour if the dough is too sticky or more water if too dry.

4 Roll out the dough out between two sheets of baking paper to about a 5 mm thickness. Partially cook in the oven at 220°C for 10 minutes, turning over halfway through, (5 minutes each side). Remove from the oven so you can add your toppings.

SAUCE

5 Mix together the Homemade Ketchup, oregano and onion powder and spread over the semi cooked pizza base.

TOPPINGS

6 Top the pizza with sliced onions and mushrooms.

7 Halve the kalamata olives and tear the prosciutto and cheese into small pieces and add onto the pizza with the basil leaves.

8 Sprinkle over the garlic powder and drizzle or spray the pizza with a little olive oil.

9 Place in the oven and cook at 220°C for 10 to 15 minutes until cooked.

CHEESE

EASY
PREP: 10 MINUTES
COOKING: 10 MINUTES
SETTING: 3 to 4 HOURS
SERVES 4
SAUCEPAN, WHISK & SILICONE MOULDS

This is such a great alternative when you fancy a cheesy, salty nibble. It doesn't melt in the same way as cheddar, but it is still so satisfying enjoyed with cold meats, olives and pickles, or as a tangy pizza topping.

Hint: To make different flavour cheeses you can stir in finely chopped apricots, serrano ham, fresh or dried herbs at the end of stage 2.

INGREDIENTS

2 TBSP extra virgin olive oil

1 cup coconut milk

3 tsp nutritional yeast

¼ tsp salt

1 to 2 tsp apple cider vinegar (depending on personal taste)

¼ tsp turmeric powder

½ tsp onion powder

½ tsp garlic powder

½ cup tapioca starch

½ fresh apricot peeled and chopped (optional)

1 TBSP gelatine powder

COOKING STEPS

1. In a saucepan add 1 TBSP olive oil, coconut milk, nutritional yeast, salt, apple cider vinegar, turmeric, onion and garlic powders and tapioca starch and stir to combine.
2. Cook over a low heat for 4–5 minutes, whisking thoroughly until the tapioca starch is cooked and the sauce thickens. Add the gelatine and whisk thoroughly until completely dissolved.
3. Pour the cheese mixture into a silicone mould lined with the remaining olive oil. Let the cheese set in the fridge for approximately 3 to 4 hours or overnight.
4. Once set remove from mould, slice and enjoy with cold meats, olives and pickles.

KAI'S FLATBREAD POCKETS

MEDIUM

PREP: 15 MINUTES
COOKING: 35 MINUTES

SERVES 8

LARGE SHALLOW FRYING PAN OR PANCAKE PAN

My son loves making filled flatbreads made from semolina flour so we thought we would try an AIP version. He helped to create this recipe, it was given the thumbs up and the leftovers were even eaten for lunch the next day.

Hint: These are perfect for a lunch on the go and are just as tasty eaten cold. They also work really well with shredded cooked chicken too.

—*Sue*

INGREDIENTS

FLATBREADS

8 Rotis (cooked) (refer to Roti recipe)

CHEESE SAUCE

8 to 10 TBSP Cheese Sauce (refer to Cheese Sauce recipe)

FILLING

3 to 4 mushrooms finely diced

4 spring onions finely sliced

120g prosciutto torn into small pieces

1 handful of baby spinach

COOKING STEPS

1 Preheat your oven to 180°C (fan) and line a tray with baking paper.

FLATBREADS

2 Refer to Roti recipe to make 8 servings.

CHEESE SAUCE

3 Refer to the Cheese Sauce recipe for method. (This recipe only requires a serving of 8 to 10 tablespoons).

FILLING

4 Divide your filling ingredients into 8 portions or average by eye if this works for you. In the centre of each roti / flatbread place your filling ingredients starting with 1 TBSP of the cheese sauce first. Add the diced mushrooms, spring onions and prosciutto and top with a few leaves of baby spinach.

5 Fold each side of the flatbread into the centre, overlapping the edges like an envelope, so the filling is held in the central pocket.

6 Turn the pocket over and place on a baking tray. Once all of the flatbreads are filled and placed onto the baking tray transfer to the oven to bake for 10 minutes until hot and crispy.

SOUPS

FRAGRANT STEAMED CHICKEN BALLS IN BONE BROTH

MEDIUM
PREP: 15 MINUTES
COOKING: 15 MINUTES
SERVES 2
GRATER, BLENDER OR FOOD PROCESSER, STEAMER OR SAUCEPAN WITH COLANDER & LID

This dish is so light and fragrant but leaves you feeling content and comforted, and it managed to satisfy my craving for wonton soup! It is perfect for a cleansing meal and is served with homemade bone broth that has been made by slow cooking chicken bones and herbs in water for 24 hours.

Hint: This dish can be served with raw vegetables such as shredded carrots, Chinese cabbage or finely sliced radishes. The chicken can be replaced with pork or a mixture of pork and prawns and either steamed and served without the broth with a dip or dusted with cassava flour and pan fried for a crispier outer coating. If serving the balls crispy, mix the juice and rind of ½ lime with 1 TBSP coconut aminos, ½ TBSP fish sauce, 1 TSP finely chopped ginger and ½ of a finely chopped shallot for a tasty dip.

INGREDIENTS

STEAMED BALLS

400g chicken thigh fillets blended
1 TBSP lemongrass blended
3 cloves garlic blended
2 shallots blended
1 TBSP ginger blended
1 TBSP coconut aminos
1 ½ TBSP fish sauce
Handful of fresh coriander
1 ½ TBSP cassava flour
2 TBSP olive oil for shaping balls

BONE BROTH

800 ml chicken bone broth
2 shallots finely chopped
3 cloves garlic finely chopped
1 TBSP lemongrass finely chopped
1 TBSP ginger finely chopped
3 kaffir lime leaves whole
3 mushrooms finely sliced or a small handful of straw mushrooms
1 TBSP coconut aminos
1 ½ TBSP fish sauce
Large handful of baby spinach
½ lime juiced and zested
Small handful of fresh coriander chopped
Small handful of fresh mint chopped
2 spring onions finely chopped

COOKING STEPS

STEAMED BALLS

1. Chop the chicken thighs into 2 cm pieces and mince to a smooth paste using a blender. Decant into a clean bowl and set aside. Chop the ends off your lemongrass and remove any tough outer skin. Bash with a rolling pin and chop into small 1 cm pieces along with the peeled garlic, shallots and ginger. Add into the same blender and blend until finely chopped. Next add the coconut aminos and fish sauce to the blender and add the minced chicken back in with the chopped coriander and cassava flour. The cassava flour should thicken the mixture, enabling the balls to hold their shape when steamed. You may require slightly more or less flour at this stage. Blend until all of the ingredients have combined well. Using a spatula stir the mixture to gauge the consistency and add in more cassava flour if the mixture appears too loose to shape into balls.
2. Lightly oil the base of your steamer or colander using your hands and set up your steamer or saucepan with colander to heat up. Using lightly oiled hands shape the mixture into small 3 cm balls and place on a lightly oiled plate. At this point the balls can be refrigerated if you are only cooking a small amount or steamed in batches for 15 minutes. The balls should change colour from pink to cream once cooked. To test if cooked cut open one of the balls which should look cream in colour and should have a firm texture.

BONE BROTH

3. Whilst the chicken balls are steaming add the bone broth into a saucepan to boil with the shallots, garlic, lemongrass, ginger, kaffir lime leaves, mushrooms, coconut aminos & fish sauce. Cover with a lid and once boiling, then lower the heat to a simmer. Add the spinach, lime zest and juice and stir. Serve with the steamed chicken balls & garnish with fresh mint, coriander and spring onion.

SHANE'S BUTTERNUT SQUASH SOUP

EASY

PREP: 15 MINUTES
COOKING: 1 HOUR

SERVES 4

MEDIUM SAUCEPAN, HAND BLENDER OR FOOD PROCESSOR

My lovely friend Shane Johnson is a professional chef and when he and his wife came to stay, he gave me a lesson in soup-making and balancing flavours. Some of the spices were off limits for AIP, but this version is still delicious.

It's smooth and creamy and easy to prepare, comforting and warming on a cold day. *—Claire*

Hint: This dish also works using frozen butternut squash. For a little extra flavour you can add 1/2 tsp mace powder or 3 curry leaves at stage 2.

INGREDIENTS

1 TBSP olive oil

2 onions peeled and chopped

1 carrot peeled and chopped

2 whole butternut squashes peeled and cubed

1 thumb size piece ginger peeled and chopped

2 garlic cloves peeled and chopped

1 can coconut milk (400ml)

1 litre bone broth (refer to Bone Broth recipe)

Salt to taste

COOKING STEPS

1. Heat the oil in your saucepan to a medium heat. Add the onions, carrots and butternut squash and allow to cook for 15 minutes, stirring occasionally until beautiful golden caramelisation occurs.
2. Add the ginger and garlic, coconut milk and bone broth and allow to simmer with the lid on for 40 minutes.
3. Remove from the stove and blend the soup to a smooth consistency using a hand blender or food processor.
4. Season, stir and serve!

AIP TOM KHA GAI – CHICKEN COCONUT SOUP

EASY

PREP: 15 MINUTES
COOKING: 20 MINUTES

SERVES 2

LARGE PAN

This delicious traditional Thai favourite is so easy. You can eat it as a soup or with steamed vegetables and other family members can spoon it over basmati rice like a curry.

For the family add 1 tomato chopped into 6 or 8 pieces and 1–2 red chillies sliced in half.

INGREDIENTS

1 can coconut milk (400ml)

1 inch galangal (you can substitute fresh ginger) peeled and sliced

2 lemongrass stalks, split lengthwise

2 cups chicken bone broth

400g chicken breast chopped into medium chunks

200g button or oyster mushrooms

1 white onion sliced

6 kaffir lime leaves torn or crumpled

Salt to taste

3 TBSP chopped fresh coriander to garnish

4 TBSP fresh lime juice

COOKING STEPS

1 In a large pan over a medium heat add the coconut milk. Stir gently and don't boil too vigorously. Throw in the galangal and lemongrass and allow them to release their flavours (you won't be eating these).

2 Add the chicken bone broth and bring to a gentle boil.

3 Meanwhile, chop the chicken breasts into medium-sized chunks and add to the coconut milk. Once this is boiling immediately turn down the heat to a simmer. Add the mushrooms and the onion slices.

4 Tear or crumple the kaffir lime leaves to release the flavour and add to the pot and season with salt to taste.

5 Cook for 10 to 15 minutes on a gentle simmer until the chicken is cooked. Then add the chopped coriander and lime juice and stir gently. Check the flavour is both salty and sour enough for your taste buds. For more salty taste add salt, for more sour add more lime juice.

6 At this point if you are sharing this meal with family or friends, set aside your portion and keep warm. To the remaining soup add the tomato pieces and the sliced chilis and cook gently for a further 5 minutes.

7 Serve as it is or with steamed vegetables. Your guests can spoon over basmati rice for more of a curry experience.

PUMPKIN & PRAWN SOUP WITH ROASTED SWEDE

MEDIUM

PREP: 15 MINUTES
COOKING: 45 MINUTES

SERVES 4

ROASTING TIN, OVEN, LARGE SAUCEPAN, HAND BLENDER OR FOOD PROCESSOR & SMALL FRYING PAN

This colourful warming soup has a few components but is well worth the wait.

Hint: This dish also works using roasted celeriac instead of swede.

INGREDIENTS

SWEDE

1 swede peeled and cubed

1 TBSP olive oil

1 TBSP garlic powder

Salt to taste

SOUP

2 TBSP olive oil

1 onion sliced

1 TBSP ginger peeled and chopped

4 garlic cloves finely chopped

1 TBSP sage finely chopped

1 small pumpkin peeled and cubed

1 litre chicken bone broth (refer to Bone Broth recipe)

1 grapefruit zested (optional)

1 can coconut milk (400ml)

Salt to taste

PRAWNS

1 TBSP olive oil

175g large raw peeled prawns

½ tsp turmeric powder

1 TBSP garlic powder

Salt to taste

3 TBSP fresh coriander chopped

COOKING STEPS

SWEDE

1. Preheat your oven to 180°C (fan). Peel and chop your swede into 2 cm cubes and place into a large mixing bowl. Drizzle over olive oil, garlic powder and salt. Mix thoroughly, decant into a roasting tin and place in the middle of the oven to cook for 40 minutes.

SOUP

2. Heat the oil in your saucepan on a low heat. Add the onions and ginger and allow to cook for 10 minutes, stirring occasionally until a beautiful golden caramelisation occurs.
3. Add the garlic and sage, frying gently for 1 to 2 minutes. Next add the pumpkin, coconut milk, bone broth and salt and allow to simmer gently with the lid on for 40 minutes.
4. Remove from the stove, add the grapefruit zest (optional) and blend soup to a smooth consistency using a hand blender or food processor.

PRAWNS

5. While the soup is cooking dry your prawns and coat in turmeric, garlic powder and salt. Heat the oil in your frying pan to a medium heat and fry the prawns for 7 to 10 minutes, turning halfway to cook both sides evenly. Garnish with fresh coriander.
6. Serve the soup and top with the roasted swede and cooked prawns.

ASPARAGUS, LEEK & ROCKET SOUP

EASY
PREP: 10 MINUTES
COOKING: 30 MINUTES
SERVES 4
LARGE SAUCEPAN & HAND BLENDER

A vibrant green and comforting vegetable soup to warm you from the inside out, made from just a few simple ingredients.

Hint: As another option you may like to add spinach into this recipe as it also works beautifully.

INGREDIENTS

2 TBSP olive oil

1 cup shallots finely chopped

350g asparagus spears chopped

1 large white sweet potato diced (3 ½ cups)

2 leeks finely chopped

4 garlic cloves finely chopped

1 litre chicken bone broth (refer to Bone Broth recipe)

1 TBSP garlic powder

2 large handfuls rocket

COOKING STEPS

1. Heat the oil in a large saucepan. Fry the shallots for a few mins to soften. Meanwhile remove the woody ends of the asparagus, chop into small pieces and set aside.
2. Peel and dice the white sweet potato into 2cm chunks and add to the pan with the chopped leeks and garlic and fry on a medium heat for 3 to 4 minutes until the leeks have softened.
3. Add the bone broth and garlic powder and bring to the boil. Once boiling reduce the heat to a medium simmer for 10 to 12 minutes until the potatoes are cooked. (You know once they are cooked if you can easily pierce with a sharp knife).
4. Add the thicker ends of the chopped asparagus and cook on a medium heat for 3 to 5 minutes, stirring well. Next add the asparagus tips and rocket leaves for 2 to 3 minutes until softened, but still bright in colour.
5. Season generously and blend with a food processor or hand blender. Add hot water to loosen if needed. Ladle into bowls and enjoy.

CHUNKY VEGETABLE SOUP

EASY

PREP: 15 MINUTES
COOKING: 45 MINUTES

SERVES 4

LARGE SAUCEPAN

Feel great with this hearty soup packed full of nutritious vegetables. You can throw in whatever leftover veg you have for a wholesome meal.

Hint: As another option you can blend your soup if you prefer a smoother consistency. It is just as delicious.

INGREDIENTS

2 TBSP olive oil

1 leek finely chopped

1 onion finely chopped

1 TBSP ginger

4 garlic cloves finely chopped

½ to 1 TBSP turmeric

1 TBSP curry leaves chopped

1 TBSP dried fenugreek leaves

1 cup carrots peeled and cubed

2 sticks celery finely chopped

1 cup swede peeled and cubed

1 cup parsnip peeled and cubed

1 cup white sweet potato peeled and cubed

800ml bone broth

1 can coconut milk (400ml)

1 cup cauliflower florets chopped

1 TBSP garlic powder

1 TBSP coconut aminos

1 TBSP fish sauce

Salt to taste

2 TBSP tapioca starch mixed with 2 TBSP water to thicken (optional)

1 lime juiced

3 TBSP fresh coriander chopped

COOKING STEPS

1 Heat the oil in a large pan and cook the leek and onion for 5 minutes until soft. Add the ginger, garlic, turmeric (to your taste), curry and fenugreek leaves and cook for 2 to 3 minutes or until fragrant.

2 Add the carrots, celery, swede, parsnip and sweet potato and cook for 10 minutes until slightly softened.

3 Add the bone broth, coconut milk and cauliflower florets and cook on a gentle simmer for 15 to 20 minutes or until all or the vegetables are cooked.

4 Season with garlic powder, coconut aminos, fish sauce and salt. If a thicker consistency is desired add tapioca starch mixed with 2 TBSP water and cook for a further 3 to 5 minutes until the tapioca starch is cooked and the soup thickens slightly.

5 Add the lime juice to taste and stir. Sprinkle over fresh coriander and serve.

TREATS & DRINKS

COOKIES

EASY
PREP: 15 MINUTES
COOKING: 15 MINUTES
SERVES APPROX. 12
SAUCEPAN & OVEN

These cookies are delightful and provide that little something when you are in need of a little sweet treat. They are surprisingly filling and perfect for sharing and with the addition of carob powder are a great alternative to chocolate cookies. For additional flavours food grade essential oils, vanilla seeds and desiccated coconut work perfectly.

INGREDIENTS

1 cup cassava flour

¼ cup coconut flour

1 pinch salt

½ cup coconut oil melted

⅓ cup maple syrup

1 tsp vanilla seeds

VARIETIES

CHOCOLATE

2 TBSP carob powder

CHOCOLATE ORANGE

2 TBSP carob powder

7 to 10 drops food grade orange essential oil

MINT CHOCOLATE

2 TBSP carob powder

7 to 10 drops food grade peppermint essential oil

LEMON

7 to 10 drops food grade lemon essential oil

COCONUT

2 TBSP desiccated coconut

COOKING STEPS

1. Preheat your oven to 170°C (fan) and line a tray with baking paper.
2. Mix the cassava flour, coconut flour and salt together in a bowl.
3. In a saucepan melt the coconut oil. Transfer this to a glass bowl and mix the melted coconut oil, maple syrup and vanilla seeds. Add the dry ingredients to the wet ingredients and mix well. The mixture should resemble a wet sand consistency. (You may need more or less coconut oil depending on the brand of your cassava flour).
4. Evenly divide the mixture and shape into 12 small round balls using your hands. Place the cookie mixture in the palm of one hand and use the base of the other to flatten the mixture into a cookie shape. Place onto the baking tray, ensuring they are evenly spaced out.
5. Bake in the oven for 15 minutes a 170°C. Once cooked and cool enough to handle, serve and enjoy, (they are especially amazing when warm!)
6. This recipe delivers a basic vanilla cookie and is great on its own or also a good base for adding additional flavours. For lemon cookies try adding lemon food grade essential oil or desiccated coconut for coconut cookies. For a chocolate flavour carob powder is perfect and by combining this with either orange or peppermint food grade essential oil delivers a chocolate orange or mint chocolate flavour.

JELLY TREATS

EASY
PREP: 5 MINUTES
COOKING: 15 MINUTES
SETTING: 2 to 4 HOURS
SERVES 10
BLENDER, SAUCEPAN, WHISK & SILICONE MOULDS

These are so much fun to make and eat and takes you back to being a child, waiting for the jelly to set. They are surprisingly refreshing and provide a touch of sweetness in your day.

Hint: These can be made using frozen or fresh fruit in a number of different combinations such as mango, lemon and mint, strawberry, lime and mint or raspberry, lime and mint.

INGREDIENTS

1 cup fruit chopped

1 citrus fruit juiced (⅛ cup)

⅛ cup water

1 TBSP fresh mint leaves

2 TBSP maple syrup

¼ cup gelatine powder

1 drop of food grade lemon or orange essential oil

STRAWBERRY, LIME & MINT

Fruit: 1 cup strawberries chopped

Juice: 1 lime juiced (⅛ cup)

MANGO, LEMON & MINT

Fruit: 1 cup mango chopped

Juice: 1 lemon juiced (⅛ cup)

RASPBERRY, LIME & MINT

Fruit:1 cup raspberries chopped

Juice: 1 lime juiced (⅛ cup)

COOKING STEPS

1. Blend your fruit, lime or lemon juice, water and mint leaves until smooth and pour into a saucepan. Add the maple syrup and gelatine powder and whisk until a thick jam-like consistency is achieved.
2. Cook on a low heat for 5 to 10 minutes, continuously whisking until the gelatine dissolves and the mixture thins. If using essential oils add them into the mixture at this point and stir with a metal spoon. Pour the mixture carefully into silicone moulds and refrigerate for a minimum of 2 hours, or overnight until set.
3. Once set carefully remove from the moulds and enjoy.

CAROB TRUFFLES

EASY
PREP: 15 MINUTES
COOKING: 20 to 30 MINUTES
SERVES 4
FORK & 3 BOWLS

These carob truffles are so creamy and with the addition of carob powder, maple syrup and vanilla, you feel like you are indulging in a luxurious chocolate truffle.

Hint: You can adapt the flavour by adding food grade essential oils such as orange or peppermint for a chocolate orange or mint chocolate flavour.

INGREDIENTS

TRUFFLES

2 medium ripe avocados

4 TBSP coconut oil melted

2 TBSP carob powder

½ tsp vanilla seeds

1 ½ TBSP maple syrup

FLAVOURINGS

½ TBSP desiccated coconut

2 drops food grade peppermint essential oil

2 drops food grade orange essential oil

¼ tsp cinnamon powder

1 TBSP carob powder for dusting

STEPS

1. Cut the avocados in half and carefully remove the stones. Scoop out the flesh with a spoon and mash with a fork until smooth.
2. Add 3 TSBP melted coconut oil, carob powder, vanilla seeds and maple syrup and stir to fully combine the mixture, turning it dark brown.
3. Divide the mixture into three and place into three separate bowls. In the first bowl place 2 drops of food grade peppermint essential oil, in the second bowl place 2 drops of food grade orange essential oil and the third bowl place ¼ tsp cinnamon powder. Mix each combination well.
4. Using your hands, coating your palms in the remaining melted coconut oil, roll a quarter of the mixture between your palms to form four small balls from each batch. Once the balls are formed roll them in carob powder and sprinkle a little desiccated coconut on top if desired. Refrigerate for 20 to 30 minutes until a little firmer in texture and enjoy.

HONEYCOMB SPRINKLES

EASY
PREP: 5 MINUTES
COOKING: 15 MINUTES
SETTING: 1 to 2 HOURS
1 SMALL JAR
SAUCEPAN & ROASTING TIN

These honeycomb sprinkles are soft and bubbly and perfect served with coconut yogurt or fruit.

INGREDIENTS

1 TBSP coconut oil for greasing the tin

100g coconut sugar

¼ tsp vanilla seeds

3 TBSP maple syrup

1 tsp bicarbonate of soda

COOKING STEPS

1. Grease a small tin with coconut oil. Stir the coconut sugar, vanilla seeds and maple syrup together in a deep saucepan over a gentle heat until the sugar has melted. Try not to let the mixture bubble until the sugar grains have disappeared.
2. Once completely melted you should have a dark golden coloured caramel (this won't take long). As quickly as you can remove the pan from the heat, add in the bicarbonate of soda and beat in with a wooden spoon until it has all disappeared and the mixture has lightened in colour and is foaming. Carefully scrape the mixture into the tin as it will be very hot.
3. Leave the mixture in the tin and refrigerate to cool completely. After 1 to 2 hours the honeycomb will have hardened slightly and can be crumbled into small chunks, which can be stored in a clean jam jar in the fridge.

APPLE & PEAR CRUMBLE WITH CUSTARD

EASY

PREP: 10 MINUTES
COOKING: 30 to 35 MINUTES

SERVES 4

SAUCEPAN & WHISK

This apple crumble with homemade custard is so homely and deliciously sweet, warm and comforting. It is such a classic dish that is guaranteed to be a real family favourite.

Crumble hint: Bake the crumble separately to achieve a toasty, nutty flavour and assemble onto the fruit before serving. In the last 3 minutes of baking, you may want to add 1 TBSP desiccated coconut to the crumble mix to toast—this is purely optional.

Custard trick: Add a pinch of turmeric powder for a custard-like appearance. It is such a small quantity so you won't tase it.

INGREDIENTS

FRUIT

230g apples (peeled and cored)

230g pears (peeled and cored)

30g coconut sugar

1 tsp cinnamon

1 lemon zested

¼ cup water (optional)

CRUMBLE

½ cup cassava flour

¼ cup coconut flour

½ tsp vanilla seeds

½ tsp cinnamon powder

1½ TBSP maple syrup

½ cup coconut oil melted

1 TBSP desiccated coconut (optional)

CUSTARD

1 can coconut milk (400ml)

1 tsp vanilla seeds

2 TBSP maple syrup

⅛ tsp turmeric (small pinch)

4 tsp arrowroot starch mixed with 2 TBSP water

COOKING STEPS

1 Preheat your oven to 170°C (fan).

FRUIT

2 Peel, core and slice or chop the apples and pears and place in a saucepan. Add the coconut sugar, cinnamon powder and lemon zest and cook on a medium heat with the lid on for 5 to 7 minutes until the fruit has softened. If you like your fruit more stewed add in ¼ cup of water with the coconut sugar and cook for slightly longer.

CRUMBLE

3 Combine the cassava flour, coconut flour, vanilla seeds, cinnamon and maple syrup. Add the melted coconut oil slowly until it forms a wet sand-like consistency. (You may need more or less coconut oil depending on the brand of your cassava flour).

4 Line an oven tray with baking paper and sprinkle with the crumble, taking care to separate any large chunks. Cook in the oven at 170°C for 10 to 12 minutes.

CUSTARD

5 In a saucepan add the coconut milk, vanilla seeds, maple syrup and turmeric. Cook on a low to medium heat for 5 to 7 minutes, whisking until fully combined.

6 Add 2 TBSP water and the arrowroot starch to the empty can of coconut milk and swirl gently. Add into the custard, cooking on a low to medium heat, whisking gently for 5 to 7 minutes until the starch is cooked and the custard has thickened. (You may need to add more water or arrowroot starch depending on your desired custard consistency).

7 Serve the cooked fruit and crumble with the warm custard and enjoy.

CAROB AND VANILLA MILK

EASY

10 MINUTES

SERVES 2

SAUCEPAN & WHISK

This drink is the perfect AIP version of hot chocolate and with warming cinnamon and the comforting taste of vanilla, it tastes like such a treat!

Hint: It can easily be modified with the addition of food grade orange essential oil to achieve a warming chocolate orange drink.

INGREDIENTS

2 cups coconut milk

1 TBSP carob powder

½ tsp vanilla seeds

½ tsp cinnamon powder

1 tsp maple syrup

1 TBSP arrowroot powder mixed with 1 tsp water

2 drops of food grade orange essential oil (optional)

STEPS

1. Heat the coconut milk, carob powder, vanilla seeds, cinnamon powder and maple syrup on a gentle simmer for 6 to 7 minutes, whisking slowly.
2. Once all of the ingredients are combined mix 1 TBSP arrowroot powder with 1 tsp water and add to the pan, whisking continuously until it reaches the desired consistency for your drink. This should take around 2 to 3 minutes.
3. If using essential oils add in at this stage and stir.
4. Pour into your favourite mug and enjoy every last sip.

GOLDEN MILK

EASY
10 MINUTES
SERVES 2
SAUCEPAN, SIEVE OR TEA STRAINER

This golden milk is so good for you and with the addition of cinnamon, maple syrup or honey it tastes great too. It is worth noting that the food grade black pepper essential oil can be omitted but if retained will increase absorption of the turmeric.

Hint: This is great for preparing in bulk as it can keep in the fridge for up to five days.

INGREDIENTS

2 cups coconut milk

1 tsp turmeric powder

½ tsp ginger powder

½ tsp cinnamon powder

1 drop food grade black pepper essential oil

1 tsp honey or maple syrup (optional—to your taste)

STEPS

1. Put all of the ingredients into a saucepan and bring to the boil.
2. Reduce the temperature and simmer for 7 to 8 minutes until fragrant, stirring occasionally.
3. Pour through a sieve or tea strainer into a mug and enjoy.

SPRITZERS

EASY

10 MINUTES

SERVES 1

SAUCEPAN, BLENDER & SIEVE

These spritzers are fresh, fruity and incredibly thirst quenching and look like sunshine in a glass. They can be made using fresh or frozen fruit—just be sure to drink these with a meal to maintain blood sugar balance.

Hint: The puree can be made in larger quantities with the maple syrup and stored in the fridge—ready to add your sparkling water whenever you like.

INGREDIENTS

STRAWBERRY & MINT

100g strawberries

5 fresh mint leaves (plus 2 leaves to garnish)

1 TBSP lemon juice

1 tsp maple syrup

½ cup sparkling water

1 handful of ice cubes

MANGO & LIME

100g mango

5 fresh mint leaves (plus 2 leaves to garnish)

½ lime juiced

1 tsp maple syrup

½ cup sparkling water

1 handful of ice cubes

CHERRY & ORANGE

60g dark sweet cherries pitted

60g orange peeled, deseeded and chopped

1 pinch cinnamon

1 TBSP water

1 tsp maple syrup

½ cup sparkling water

1 handful of ice cubes

1 orange slice to garnish

STEPS

1. Add fruit, herbs or spice and citrus juice or water (as required) to a small saucepan. Cook for 2 to 3 minutes over medium heat to soften and infuse.
2. Place the contents of the pan into a blender and blitz to a smooth puree.
3. Sieve the puree using a tea strainer into a clean glass, add maple syrup and sparkling water and stir. Add ice cubes and garnish and serve immediately.

SMOOTHIES

EASY
5 to 10 MINUTES
SERVES 1
BLENDER

These creamy and refreshing smoothies are so quick to make and can be made from frozen fruit or your favourite fresh fruit and vitamin-packed veg. Just be sure to drink these with a meal to maintain blood sugar balance.

INGREDIENTS

PINA COLADA

100g frozen pineapple
½ cup coconut milk
3 mint leaves
1 tsp maple syrup
½ cup sparkling water

RASPBERRY & PEAR

100g frozen raspberries
1 pear peeled, cored and chopped
1 tsp ginger peeled and roughly chopped
½ cup coconut milk
1 tsp maple syrup
½ cup sparkling water

SPINACH & APPLE

50g Spinach
½ lime peeled, deseeded and chopped
1 apple peeled, cored and chopped
1 cup cucumber chopped
5 mint leaves
1 tsp maple syrup
½ cup sparkling water

STEPS

1. Place all of the ingredients into a blender and blitz until smooth.
2. Pour into a glass and serve immediately.

APPENDICES

APPENDIX 1

Conversion Charts

Oven Temperatures

°C	°F	Gas Mark
260	500	10
240	475	9
230	450	8
220	425	7
200	400	6
190	375	5
180	350	4
170	325	3
150	300	2
140	275	1
120	250	½
110	225	¼

For fan ovens reduce temperature by 20°C or 65°F

Fluid Ounce (fl oz) to Millilitres (ml)

fl oz	ml
1 fl oz	28 ml
2 fl oz	57 ml
3 fl oz	85 ml
4 fl oz	114 ml
5 fl oz	142 ml
6 fl oz	170 ml
7 fl oz	199 ml
8 fl oz	227 ml
9 fl oz	256 ml
10 fl oz	284 ml

Grams (g) to Ounces (oz)

g	oz
1 g	0.04 oz
2 g	0.07 oz
3 g	0.11 oz
4 g	0.14 oz
5 g	0.18 oz
6 g	0.21 oz
7 g	0.25 oz
8 g	0.28 oz
9 g	0.32 oz
10 g	0.35 oz
20 g	0.71 oz
30 g	1.06 oz
40 g	1.41 oz
50 g	1.76 oz
60 g	2.12 oz
70 g	2.47 oz
80 g	2.82 oz
90 g	3.17 oz
100 g	3.52 oz

Cups / Millilitres (ml)

Cups (UK)	ml
⅛ cup	30 ml
¼ cup	60 ml
⅓ cup	75 ml
½ cup	125 ml
⅔ cup	150 ml
¾ cup	175ml
1 cup	250 ml
2 cups	500 ml
3 cups	750 ml
4 cups	1000 ml (1 litre)

Spoons: Millilitres (ml), Teaspoon (tsp) and Tablespoon (TBSP)

ml	tsp / TBSP
1.25 ml	¼ tsp
2.5 ml	½ tsp
5 ml	1 tsp
10 ml	2 tsp
15 ml	1 TBSP
30 ml	2 TBSP
45 ml	3 TBSP

APPENDIX 2

Some Science Behind the Exclusions

As I said at the start, the aim with this book is not to provide information to fill your head—that doesn't lead to transformation—implementing what you learn is how you change your health for the better and so most of this book is designed to help you get into action and move past obstacles.

That said, I know that you might need some science to back up the changes you intend to make to your diet. I have two Bachelor of Science degrees so I certainly can relate to the thirst for knowledge.

In this appendix I will give you some of the high level reasons why you exclude certain foods. Many of them have a lot of nutritional merit and you will want to have them back on your plate once your gut has healed and your immune system has become more regulated. Other foods—well there's not a lot of goodness in them and you may decide to part company for good.

If you are looking for a more in-depth, scientific underpinning of the AIP diet, then I once again recommend *The Paleo Approach* by Sarah Ballantyne PhD. She is arguably the most knowledgeable person on nutrient density, gut health, and AIP. One caveat—do not let your mental appetite for knowledge postpone your implementation of the AIP diet—start feeling better now.

Grains

These foods have many components that are problematic for those with gut issues and autoimmune disease.

Firstly, they contain lectins which are "anti-nutrient" proteins. The specific **lectins** we want to avoid are **prolamins** and **agglutinins**, which we do not digest. They further impair digestion, cross the gut barrier largely in their complete form, damage the intestinal lining (causing increased intestinal permeability also known as leaky gut) and ramp up the immune system.

The presence of these types of lectins also contribute to an overgrowth of harmful bacteria (dysbiosis) by inhibiting your digestive enzymes, meaning you cannot readily break down the food you are consuming. Anything you can't digest, is more food for potentially pathogenic bacteria and yeast further down the digestive tract.

As well as lectins, grains also contain other **digestive enzyme inhibitors, phytates** and **phytic acid**, (all anti-nutrients, or substances that interfere with the absorption of food). These anti-nutrients survive cooking, resist digestion and contribute to leaky gut, dysbiosis, and worsen immune activation.

The toxic and immune-stimulating effects of these components in grains makes it very clear that for those seeking to heal a leaky gut, regulate their immune system and reduce inflammation, these foods should not be consumed.

Gluten

A component of gluten found in grains (wheat, barley, and rye specifically) known as **gliadin** is the best-known example of a **prolamin** (a type of **lectin**). Specifically, gliadin fragments cross the gut barrier, and once inside the body, these protein fragments stimulate the immune system. Through this process, gliadin causes damage to the gut lining, which results in the creation of holes in the gut barrier through which various contents of the digestive system can leak into the body.

Inflammation is triggered by gliadin fragments that cross the gut barrier, as well as by other partially digested food proteins, gut bacteria, bacterial fragments, and waste products, like toxins, crossing over into the body through the holes created by gliadin. All of this activates the immune system, causing a vicious cycle of inflammation and gut-barrier damage, and is why the gluten-containing grains (wheat, barley and rye) are typically the most problematic for those with gut issues or autoimmune disease and probably a food never reintroduced successfully.

Grains contain many proteins which may have a similar effect to gluten but haven't been as fully investigated. Gluten has just been studied in the most depth because it is a direct cause of Coeliac Disease.

Pseudo-grains and Grain-like Substances

Pseudo-grains include things like quinoa, buckwheat and chia. Although these are not true grains, they contain many of the same substances that impair the digestive process, cause leaky gut, worsen gut dysbiosis and activate the immune system: **lectins** (such as **prolamins** and **agglutinins**), **digestive enzyme inhibitors, phytates** and **phytic acid**. In addition, pseudo-grains can also contain **saponins**, which have detergent-like qualities also shown to damage the delicate intestinal barrier.

When reintroducing pseudo-grains, the phytic acid levels can be reduced by soaking and rinsing them prior to cooking.

Dairy

There are many reasons why a person with gut issues or autoimmune disease would want to avoid dairy products. First, dairy is a common **allergenic food**, affecting mostly children but also many adults (estimates are in the range of 1–17% of the population). For the people with dairy allergies to the milk protein, **casein**, even trace proteins in ghee can be a problem.

Additionally, 25–75% of people (depending on ethnicity) are unable to digest **lactose**, a sugar found in milk.

Dairy products contain **digestive enzyme inhibitors** that may contribute to leaky gut.

Dairy products are highly insulinogenic, which may contribute to inflammation and **insulin resistance**; they contain active hormones which have the potential to alter human hormone levels and they increase mucus production, which can irritate the gut lining and hinder nutrient absorption, further exacerbating nutrient deficiencies.

Lastly, cow's milk proteins are also known to be gluten cross-reactors, which means that if someone is sensitive to gluten, these dairy proteins may stimulate a person's immune system in exactly the same way, as if they were eating gluten.

Legumes (beans, peas and pulses)

Like grains and pseudo-grains, legumes contain many of the same substances that impair the digestive process, cause leaky gut, worsen gut dysbiosis, and activate the immune system, such as **lectins** (like **prolamins** and **agglutinins**), **digestive enzyme inhibitors, phytates** and **phytic acid**.

In addition, legumes can also contain **saponins**, which have detergent-like qualities and are similarly damaging to the intestinal barrier.

Processed Vegetable and Seed Oils

Omega-6 fatty acids are concentrated in modern, processed vegetable oils which raises inflammation in our bodies, initiating many chronic inflammatory diseases, including autoimmune disease.

A balanced dietary ratio of **Omega-6** to **Omega-3**, between 1:1 and 4:1, is optimal for human health. Use of these Omega-6 oils creates a ratio of anywhere from 25:1 to 100:1.

Additionally, the manufacturing process to produce these oils results in toxic end-products, forming **free radicals**. These altered fatty acid molecules damage DNA, RNA, cell membranes, blood vessel walls and red blood cells, all of which snowball into deeper tissue damage.

Processed food chemicals and ingredients

A number of health concerns surround the chemicals commonly added to manufactured and processed foods. Preservatives, colourings, sulphites, phosphates and emulsifiers have been shown to have a negative impact in a wide range of areas. Furthermore, sensitivities to these chemicals are common enough to suggest that avoiding foods that contain these additives is a good idea.

Added Sugars

The first problem with sugar is that it is typically added to nutritionally poor foods in order to make them **addictive**. When the body is not receiving the nutrients it needs from these empty foods, a vicious cycle results in ever higher cravings for the added sugar.

The second problem with sugar is that increased consumption leads to issues with **blood sugar regulation**, which can look like **insulin resistance, high blood sugar levels, diabetes** and **weight gain**. Regulating blood sugar levels and maintaining insulin sensitivity are critical to regulating the immune system and reducing inflammation.

Sugar Alcohols

Sugar alcohols, such as Xylitol, are fermentable sugars that are incompletely absorbed in the intestine and have been shown to disproportionately feed harmful bacteria in the gut, meaning that they have the potential to worsen gut dysbiosis.

Other studies have shown that they have the ability to increase leaky gut.

Non-nutritive Sweeteners

These compounds have been linked to increased risk of obesity and metabolic syndrome through their effect on hormones and metabolism. They have been shown to have physiological effects that alter appetite and glucose metabolism, not in a good way.

Even natural non-nutritive sweeteners, like stevia, have been shown to negatively impact hormone balance.

Other types or artificial sweeteners (like aspartame) have been shown to increase oxidative stress and inflammation in the brain. Many of the long-term effects of these chemicals are unknown.

Nuts and Seeds

Nuts and seeds contain both **digestive enzyme inhibitors** as well as **phytic acid**, which has the potential to worsen leaky gut and feed bacterial overgrowths. In addition, many nuts are common allergenic foods.

AUTHOR BIOS

CLAIRE SMEDLEY
HEALTH COACHING

Claire Smedley

Claire Smedley currently lives in Thailand with her husband Neil, after embarking on a nomadic lifestyle mid-pandemic. Selling almost everything they owned, they set off on an adventure and freed themselves from physical ties. She has one grown son, now a ski instructor in Switzerland.

Claire has always been fascinated by what it is to be human, a healthy human—in body, mind and spirit. She got her degrees in Biochemistry and Chemistry and then began to explore eastern concepts of health and wellbeing.

Following her own recovery from Hashimoto's Thyroiditis and lifelong irritable bowel syndrome, she refocussed her career to help other women who felt frustrated and disempowered by their autoimmune diseases.

After more than two decades as a yoga and meditation teacher & trainer, she now works remotely as an Integrative Nutrition Health Coach with specialisms in the Autoimmune Protocol and Gut Health, as well as subconscious reprogramming and breathwork.

Claire blends diet, lifestyle and mindset coaching to enable women to fulfil their potential, not only in their health, but in life. She works from the premise that there can be no physical health, without emotional, mental and spiritual health, aligned with an intrinsic sense of purpose, unique to each individual.

For more about her work and coaching programs, you can visit her website: www.clairesmedleyhealthcoaching.com

Or join her Facebook group: facebook.com/groups/empoweredautoimmunecommunity

Sue Persad-Patel

Sue Persad-Patel lives in the UK with her husband, two children and two cats. She delights in discovering, creating and experimenting with food and her world would not be complete without flavour.

Sue has always been creative, loved cooking and loved helping people, but it wasn't until joining Claire's programme that she realised how she could combine all three passions. After struggling with Chronic Fatigue Syndrome for many years she would love to be able to help people with autoimmune diseases to nourish themselves and to feel supported and inspired to cook exciting and mouth watering AIP dishes, helping to positively change their lives.

For more information you can visit her website: www.aipcookingwithsue.com

ACKNOWLEDGEMENTS

I would like to offer my heartfelt thanks to everyone who has supported and nagged me to write this book.

Firstly, to Sue for agreeing to collaborate on this book, without whom this would never have happened. Thank you for your mouth-watering recipes and inspiring photography. Working with you Sue, has been so much fun and so joyful!

By far, the deepest gratitude must go to my wonderful husband Neil, who has done so much in bringing this book to fruition. When, for my own recovery, I decided I would embark on the AIP diet he embraced the journey wholeheartedly. Neil, my love, you have always been my kitchen buddy, I love preparing food with you and I thank you with all my heart, that you supported my need to nourish myself this way. From adapting our everyday meals to make them AIP-compliant (I will always devour your roast chicken with gravy with gusto) to making me special foods such as tamarind chutney, liver pâté and nomato sauce so I always have staples in the fridge for ravenous moments. Thank you, my love—you make everything in life fabulous. And for surviving the constant re-reading of the drafts, I applaud your patience. xxx

Thank you, Melina Lew for your phenomenal graphic design skills which turned our humble manuscript into a feast for the eyes. It's been an absolute pleasure to work with you. Writing the book was the easy bit but the work required to bring it to a level fit for human visual consumption always felt beyond me. Thank you Bruce Bowditch, my friend, fellow yoga teacher and I can now say fellow published author, for sending me Melina's way.

I also want to thank the women in my life—my Mum and Grandmother (Mam) who I always loved to spend time with in the kitchen. Thank you, Mum, for giving me the responsibility of making gravy and custard, which remain to this day, two of my favourite comfort foods, along with your "runny nose dinner" which I wished we could have every evening during winter. Thank you, Mam, for showing me that food is an expression of love, as well as nourishment; for saying nothing, just smiling sweetly, as you watched me pick every one of those pesky currants from your delicious Welsh Cakes and never criticising. Thank you for then always making me my own set of Welsh Cakes with desiccated coconut instead of currants because you knew I didn't like them.

I am grateful for my son Finian Murphy for his willingness to try crazy new flavours—I remember you trying snails at seven years old and eating every one. I love to see your inventive kitchen creations as you step out into the world on your own two feet—you inspire me!

One unexpected and late acknowledgement goes to my wonderful sister-in-law, Sandra Colgate, for being willing to read the draft manuscript whilst on holiday visiting us—perfect timing! I hope I have inspired you to try a few new recipes. x

To all my clients and friends who have encouraged me to put pen to paper, thank you. Your journeys to health inspire me every single day. Your courage at taking back control of your health is a remarkable testament to the power of the human heart. You bring living truth to the expression "where there's a will, there's a way." I love each one of you and you always astound and inspire me to do better.

Really, this book is dedicated to every person who is willing to take hold of the reins of their own health and pursue wellbeing. You are too numerous to mention by name—but you know who you are.

—Claire

Claire, I can't begin to thank you enough for all that you have done for me. Your work has taught me so much. It has changed my life in so many positive ways and reenergised my creativity, something I truly thought I had lost. Inviting me to collaborate on this book has felt like a dream come true so thank you for the opportunity, for really seeing me and for making this so much fun that I wanted it to last forever.

Thank you to my beautiful family, my husband and children for your support and genuine love for food. I love that we all get so excited by food and when we cook together it is priceless. I could not have done this without you. Thank you to my children for your curiosity, for being my taste testers, having the last say on my photographs, for your honest feedback and for inspiring me.

Thank you to my parents for showering my sister and I with love, for creating such flavour in our lives with your food that we still crave to this day and for making food such a big part of our lives.

Trish, thank you for being the most amazing sister anyone could ask for, for giving the best advice and for always cheering me on. To me you will always be my amazing big sister.

Rachel, I will always be grateful to you for helping me to start this wonderful journey and for your continued support along the way.

To my AIP friends, thank you for being so positive, supportive and welcoming. I continue to admire you all, your determination, inner strength and courage.

Lindsay, thank you for your true understanding and connection, for helping me to believe in myself and shine again.

To my girls, my fabulous friends who I would never be without. Thank you always for your friendship, support and unconditional love.

—Sue

RECIPE INDEX

NOTES

Printed in Great Britain
by Amazon

86184487R00114